The Aerofilms Book of
BRITAIN FROM THE AIR

Overleaf The heart of Oxford.

Bernard Stonehouse

The Aerofilms Book of

BRITAIN FROM THE AIR

Foreword by
Sir Huw Wheldon

Weidenfeld & Nicolson London

First published in Great Britain by
Weidenfeld and Nicolson Ltd
91 Clapham High Street
London s w 4

Designed by Joyce Chester
Picture Editor: Julia Brown
House Editor: Lucy Shankleman
Map on p. 6 by Line and Line

Transparencies made by Obscura Ltd from original colour negatives
Typeset by Keyspools Ltd, Golborne, Lancashire
Colour separations by Newsele Litho Ltd,
Printed in Hong Kong by Mandarin Publishers Ltd

ISBN 0 297 78121 9

Foreword

Britain from the Air is well named. There are enough photographs and enough variety of scene, enough information, some of it sensational, and enough glimpses of all kinds of activity to provide an arresting, fresh and rounded impression of this wonderfully complicated and surprising country.

To see things from the air is to see them from a genuinely new point of view, and I myself believe that serious exploration into human affairs by way of aerial photography is only just starting. It is of course the case that the ceaseless flow of events can be seen afresh from any new vantage point. The problem is finding such vantage points without yielding to mere eccentricity.

'There was this eight-legged white insect swimming hard along the exact centre of the water. Behind it was another eight-legged black insect, and then a flotilla of blunt-nosed, wingless beetles.'

Thus Peter Black described a televised helicopter-eye view of the Boat Race. It was observations of this kind which led the BBC, in my time, to set up a series called *Bird's-Eye View*. I cannot claim direct parentage – I wish I could. It was a marvellous series and I was proud of it. Edward Mirzoeff produced thirteen programmes before we had to discontinue them. They were too expensive. But we learnt a lot about the possibilities and the hazards of aerial photography.

The main hazard, certainly in moving photographs, is that it often seems, in a most mysterious fashion, as if what you see when you look down from the air is something that is already over, part of all our yesterdays. To see something from above is somehow to have put it in aspic. Buildings, rivers, woodlands and roads filmed from a travelling helicopter are drowned in a shimmering, nostalgia-soaked haze. Everything is beautiful, more like a memory or a dream than something real. There lies England's green and pleasant land, forever undefiled. Even little groups of mean buildings – Nissen huts or tacky developments plonked down in the endless green

parkland – somehow suggest order and purpose, not spoliation; and much of what we see, be it excavations or high chimneys, concrete structure or industrial waste, takes its place from the air neatly and modestly, like so many copses and spinneys in the enchanted landscape.

In our television series we gradually learned to cope with the curious forces which were forever tempting us towards some form of slightly dotty sentimentality. It seemed almost as if our helicopter was providing us with a God's-Eye view as we were being privileged to take part in an inspection of his work by a benevolent creator.

James Plunkett, John Betjeman, Corelli Barnett and others helped Mirzoeff battle with these unfamiliar perspectives, and between them they distilled true insights and meanings yielded by this new material. Similarly, Dr Stonehouse has made wonderful use of the Aerofilms archives in his juxtaposition of text and pictures.

In some ways still photographs are perhaps easier to handle. Certainly you can hit the target fair and square, as in the marvellous and appalling photograph of the pile-up on the motorway (p. 131); or in the striking study of Oxford (p. 2), so full of impact and clarity. This is Oxford, now, today; and the spires dream rather less than they sometimes do from across the water-meadows.

Some of the pictures are breathtaking, but here again, the editing is judicious. Thus, the Power Stations (p. 70) floating on their cloudy beds are an entrancing vision, worth seeing in any collection of aerial photographs; but we are not likely to believe that to visit them on foot is actually to go into The Land of Eiderdown, as the photograph suggests.

The photographs have been chosen with a loving and discerning eye. They tell of a country rich with memory and meaning, used, enjoyed and celebrated by generations of men, women and children. We see ourselves anew. Treherbert (p. 45) reminds us how complex an experience of life is summed up in the words 'The Valleys'. The South Wales valleys were

never simply black country; and you could always catch glimpses between the chimneypots of green grass and ancient sheep runs. There is Hampton Court Palace with its magnificent avenues and hedges and gardens (p. 152). There is Pleshey in Essex, so contained (p. 148), and Canterbury (p. 145), suggesting the ancient fortresses which lie at the heart of so many of our cities and towns. We see Hadrian's Wall snaking along the Whin Sill, and a fort's foundations, alongside it, irreducibly Roman (p. 101).

And beyond all these layers of recorded history there are hitherto unimaginable views of the island itself, limestone and chalk and granite under sunshine and under rain. Geology, we are reminded, is the bed-rock.

This is a fascinating book, always informative, nearly always unexpected, and sometimes ravishing. I only hope that it proves to be the first in a series of further and particular explorations.

Sir Huw Wheldon

THE ROUTE

FRANCE

CHANNEL ISLANDS

ENGLISH CHANNEL

ATLANTIC OCEAN

IRELAND

IRISH SEA

NORTH SEA

Jersey
Alderney

St Michael's Mount
Red River
St Ives
Carluddon
East and West Looe
Appledore
Exeter
Haytor
Brixham
Salcombe
Chesil Beach
Osborne House
The Needles
Portsmouth
Hamble
Salisbury
Stourhead
Clevedon
Clifton Gorge
Avebury Rings
Ashdown House
Henley-on-Thames
Woking
Eton College
Little Gaddesden
Hampton Court
London
R. Thames
Chequers Court
Waddesdon Manor
Ridgmont
Milton Keynes
Deanshanger
Cambridge
Pleshey
Borough Green
Hamford Water
Wivenhoe
Aldeburgh
Orford Ness
Norwich
The Broads
Great Yarmouth
Grime's Graves
Skegness
Mablethorpe
The Wash
Boston
Corby
Weston
Leicester
Belvoir
Donington Park
Grimsby
Chesterfield
Kingston-upon-Hull
Whitby
York
Ferrybridge
Sheffield
Leek
Headingley
Manchester
Durham
Washington
North Seaton
Ashington
Farne Islands
Fountains Abbey
Raven Scar
Fiddler's Ferry
Runcorn
Liverpool
Little Moreton Hall
Chester
Birkenhead
Leyland Test Track
Blackpool
Bowness
Housesteads
Brackenthwaite Fell
Borrowtree Tarn
Ingleton
Ennerdale Water
Dumfries
Hawick
Edinburgh
Firth of Forth
Stirling University
Motherwell
Glasgow
Crinan Canal
Inveraray
Loch Lomond
Ben Nevis
Great Glen
Mallaig
West Highlands
Cuillin Hills
Dee Valley
Strathpeffer
Strathspey
Chirk Castle
Iron Bridge
Shrewsbury
Brecon Beacons
Bredwardine
Gravelly Hill
Stratford-upon-Avon
Tewkesbury
Great Malvern
Castell Dinas Bran
Bethesda
Snowdonia
Caernarfon
Menai Bridge
Conwy
Gronant
Aberdovey
Aberystwyth
Whitford Point
Tenby
Pembroke
Angle
Haverfordwest
Treherbert
Vale of Ewyas
Highgrove House
Severn Bridge
Cardiff Docks
The Dunnisbournes
Bath
Blenheim Palace
Sutton
King's
Uffington Castle
Scotney Castle
Bedgebury Pinetum
Canterbury
Westbere
Dover
Rottingdean
Glyndebourne
Beachy Head
Shoreham and Portslade

Introduction

Britain is a breakwater off the coast of Eurasia – largest of a group of low-lying islands that fringe the western European plains and hold the Atlantic Ocean and North Sea apart. In spring it turns green, in autumn dull brown; in winter its highlands wear a cope of snow that spreads to lower ground for weeks on end. Astronauts see it this way, but they seldom see it complete, for there is usually a haze of industrial smoke and a pall of cloud over Britain, even when the rest of Europe is clear.

But on watch in the evening they see it spring to life with a hundred million lights, that cut through the gloom and shine like good deeds in a dim world. Lights of homes and factories, roads, cities, villages and ubiquitous motor cars, they remind us that Britain is more than a breakwater; it is one of the most densely populated islands on earth and, whatever the economists say, one of the busiest and most prosperous after two thousand years and more of civilization.

Nature and the human population have combined to make Britain an intensely complex island, richly detailed and many-faceted. Before man arrived it was already a jumble of rocks and rivers, glaciers, mountains and plains – product of millions of years of geological turmoil in an unusually active area of the earth's crust. Already it had clothed itself in a rich variety of vegetation, with forest, grassland, swamp and moorland, but all on a tiny island scale – the whole of Britain could have fitted easily into one of the great forests of France or Germany. Man brought more textures to the tapestry with his villages and towns, crops and plantations, castles, cathedrals and canals, and laced them strongly together with a web of memories and historical associations. Spend a lifetime in Britain and you may not notice the wealth about you; spend a month in a newer country, and you'll know straight away what is missing.

Living in Britain today, under the smog and among the clutter of humanity past and present, is like living in a vast, untidy treasure garden. Within it nature is cribbed, confined, but far from subdued, and ready to take over again as soon as we are gone. Man-made things predominate; we may think of it as a natural garden, but you are seldom out of sight of a human artefact, and the countryside itself is as contrived as a rose-bed. Architectural jewels stand cheek-by-jowl with rubbish, tenth-century buildings with twentieth-century, and an Iron Age track may be bridged by last year's motorway. Tidy folk deplore all this and wonder when we are going to clear it up. Discerning visitors love it (apart from the litter and the Olde Englysh rip-offs), and pour in by the thousand to absorb it. Britons too like Britain, though we may not always say so. What else could have kept us here so long in the rain and the cold?

There is plenty to see, feel and savour in the shabby old garden of Britain, plenty to enjoy in a ramble about it, despite the patches of squalor that come from overcrowding and neglect. This book is a ramble by air – one that lifts us above the crowds and gives us a new viewpoint. *The Aerofilms Book of Britain from the Air* looks down on Britain from a thousand feet up – sometimes more, sometimes less, but always high enough to yield a new, uncluttered view of the garden – to see what Britons have made of it over the centuries.

This view of Britain was practically unknown at the start of the century. None but a few intrepid balloonists had seen it, and aerial photographs were almost unheard of. More saw it during World War I when thousands flew for the first time, and aerial photography was widely used for spotting and survey. Today it is a more familiar viewpoint. Millions glimpse Britain briefly from the air on tourist flights, but only on take-off and landing; jet aircraft fly too high for much of the ground to be seen during the flight itself. Smaller planes are better – keeping an eye on things below is half the business and more than half the fun of light aircraft flying. In this book we are taking things more gently, for we are drifting in an imaginary balloon over the length and breadth of Britain. If there is a better way of appreciating the sheer beauty of our island, I'd be glad to know it. As the photographs show,

Britain is superb from the air, like a fascinating, multi-coloured model of a half-imagined Erewhon, and there is much to be seen from a thousand feet that you would be lucky indeed to see from the ground.

Britain from the Air is based on the archives of Aerofilms Ltd, the firm that pioneered commercial aerial photography in Britain. Since 1919 Aerofilms cameramen have been photographing steadily for a dozen different purposes including many general photographs, just for the record, which are filed in an extensive library at Borehamwood. Most of the material is in black and white, and more is being added to the archive every year; several prints of historic interest are included on pages 156–7. The first colour photographs were taken in 1938, but for more than a decade now Aerofilms have been photographing regularly in colour, and the bulk of this book is made up of a selection – a very small one – from their colour material.

Almost any colour photograph taken over Britain has something arresting about it, and selecting 152 pictures from an archive of thousands was an intriguing task, as well as a frustrating one. Editor, picture editor and author worked together, seeking pictures with good visual impact and good stories behind them, and there was no shortage of either in the Aerofilms files. Another splendid castle – or have we too many already? Another Roman road striding off through the wheatfields? This White Horse or that one? Norwich or Salisbury Cathedral – or both? These dunes with the ripple marks in front, or those with the pattern of caravans behind? Britain is a fascinating land, rich beyond measure in its surface textures and patterns, and aerial photographs bring out the best for everyone to see. I hope our selection has done it justice.

Britain's basic texture is its bed-rock, underlying and setting a matrix for all the others. Standing at the edge of a continental mass, our island has suffered more than its share of geological pressures and upheavals. It gained in the process a variety of rock types from granites to soft shales; hence its varied surface texture, that reflects the differences beneath. North Americans, Australians, even northern Europeans who visit Britain marvel at the variety of scenery packed into so small a space. You can travel for two days across continental Australia or Canada and see the horizon stretching pancake-flat in every direction. Two *hours'* journey in Britain takes you from the plains of Cheshire to the peaks of Snowdonia, from rough granite moorlands to smooth chalk downs, from high crags inland to shady beaches by the sea.

The foundation of Britain is an ancient platform of hard rocks over two thousand million years old. It appears at the surface in north-west Scotland, Anglesey, and a few scattered places in the south including the Malvern Hills (p. 41). Repeatedly over millions of years this platform has dropped below sea level and accumulated layers of sediments – muds, clays, silts, sands and gravels – washed down into the sea by the erosion of nearby land masses. Each time it has risen with its load, the sediments compressed under their own weight, crimped into folds by lateral pressures, and baked by heat from the heart of the earth. Repeatedly the sediments have been eroded by wind, rain, rivers and glaciers, and then dunked again to acquire another load during the next cycle of deposition.

Some of the earliest sediments form the core of the mountains that appear to the east of the Great Glen (p. 87). They surface again in the valley of the Dee (p. 57), and make up several of the peaks that surround the massif of Ben Nevis (p. 86). Snowdonia's volcanic rocks were erupted at about the same time as these sediments were laid down, some six hundred million years ago. Later deposits of mud, perhaps five hundred million years old, were squeezed and baked to form the many-coloured slates of North Wales (p. 57), while black sands and silts produced the greywacke cliffs behind Aberystwyth and Aberdovey (pp. 52 and 53). About four hundred million years ago desert sands drifted together to form the huge sheets of Old Red Sandstone that lie beneath much of the north and west. These are responsible for the Ochil Hills behind Stirling University (p. 94), the Brecon Beacons (p. 44) and many more of Britain's most striking uplands and escarpments.

Three hundred million years ago southern Britain lay under a tropical shallow sea, accumulating layers of limestone, dense swamp vegetation and dark sandy grits. These Carboniferous deposits, more than any others, led to Britain's prosperity during the Industrial Revolution, for the lime-

stones became enriched with iron ores and the swamp vegetation turned to coal. Carboniferous deposits provide some of our fine upland scenery, including the limestone fault-escarpments of North Wales (p. 61) and North Yorkshire (pp. 74 and 75), the Clifton Gorge (p. 36) and the Millstone Grits of the Pennines near Sheffield (p. 116). The cliffs at Whitby (p. 104) are of Carboniferous limestone, laced with seams of red iron ore and delicate marine fossils. Volcanic eruptions during the same period peppered the Scottish lowlands with hard basalt cones; two of them in Edinburgh form Arthur's Seat and Castle Rock (p. 96).

Toward the end of the Carboniferous period pressures from below arched the Pennines, separating our eastern and western coalfields, and an extensive layer of basalt was injected into the limestones of northern England, forming the Whin Sill. This is the hard ridge on which the Romans built the middle section of Hadrian's Wall (p. 101). Its eastern extension forms the Farne Islands, where thousands of sea birds still build their nests every year (p. 98). Crustal movements in the south allowed the huge mushrooms of molten rock to rise under Devon and Cornwall, producing the granite massifs of Dartmoor (p. 27), St Austell (p. 29), and enriching the south-western peninsula with minerals – some of which colour the Red River at Godrevy (p. 32).

Britain's plains and rolling eastern hills are formed of softer sediments laid down in the last 250 million years, mostly in shallow seas that spread eastward far across Europe. Deposits include the clays and sandstones of the Midlands, the thick bands of salt that underlie Cheshire and the industrial north-east, and the iron-rich limestones of the Cotswolds, the Midlands and North Yorkshire. Both Cotswold stone villages (p. 39) and open-cast mining at Corby (p. 121) are based on these honey coloured Jurassic limestones: Bredon Hill is a sandy limestone knoll on a Jurassic clay plain (p. 40). Muds laid down later in the North Sea basin, rich in organic material, gave rise to the oil-bearing shales and fields of natural gas on which Britain is currently drawing. Then came the sands and clays of the Weald, and the chalk that rims it and makes up so much of the south-eastern coast (pp. 10, 12 and 17). Alpine crustal movements of twenty to thirty million years ago helped to shape both the Weald and the Isle of Wight (p. 17). Subtler, longer-lasting earth movements began to heave up the ancient massifs of hard, crystalline rock that now form the northern and western highlands. So Britain gradually acquired the shape and form we are familiar with today.

Until about two million years ago the world managed perfectly well without ice-caps. Temperate climates extended into high latitudes; crocodiles swam where polar bears live now, and Britain basked in warm-temperate to tropical climates. As little as a million and a half years ago there were coral reefs in the seas off southern Britain, and rhinoceros and hippopotamus roamed the forests of the Midlands. There were probably real lions where the stone ones stand in Trafalgar Square today. By this time, however, the ends of the earth were chilling rapidly. Permanent ice began to build up in Antarctica, the Arctic, and on high ground in Canada, Scandinavia and Britain, finally spreading across the lowland plains as well. This was the start of the Ice Age, a period of lasting cold that has affected Britain in many ways during the past million and more years.

Since the Ice Age began, climates in our latitudes have fluctuated between temperate and glacial, and Britain has been submerged repeatedly under sheets of ice well over a 1,000 metres (3,300 feet) thick. Everywhere north of the Severn and Thames has been glaciated at least once and usually more. The ice advanced from the high domes of Scotland, Cumbria and North Wales, retreating during intervening warm spells. Permanent ice last lay upon Britain less than ten thousand years ago, and only a slight cooling in our climate would be enough to bring it back with a rush.

Movements of the ice sheets were responsible for much of the detailing in our scenery – the rounding and smoothing of mountains, the shapes of valleys. They shaped, too, many curious patterns of modern river drainage that cannot be explained otherwise. These pictures show some of the effects of glaciation – the Black Mountains (p. 43) for example, and the flat, U-shaped valleys of South Wales (p. 45) and the Lake District (pp. 76, 77 and 79). The rocks of Brackenthwaite Fell (p. 78) and Mallaig (p. 88) were polished by ice, and ice smoothed the valleys where Strathpeffer stands, leaving a platform for the town (p. 91). Many of our settlements were built on compacted moraines that the glaciers left, lifting them slightly above the general level and out of the floods. Several of our rivers owe their channels to the time when the ice was melting; Ironbridge Gorge was carved, not by the sleepy old Severn (p. 63), but by a fiercer river that drained a huge glacial lake to the north, where Manchester stands today.

Sea level rose as the ice sheets melted, and salt water spread over the marshy plain that lay between Britain and the Low Countries. What had for long been the delta of a combined

Rhine and Thames river became the bed of a shallow North Sea, and Britain lay isolated from the continent. Relieved of its weight of ice the land began to rise. Parts of it – those that bore the heaviest load – continue to rise today. The Scottish Highlands are still growing taller at a rate of two or three millimetres per year, while southern and eastern England are sinking at about the same rate. Coastal drowning has produced the fine natural harbours of Portsmouth (p. 14), Salcombe (p. 24) and Hamford Water (p. 128), and contributed to the laziness of the meandering Broads rivers (p. 124).

The natural vegetation that spread to cover Britain after the last retreat of the ice matured gradually into forest. Lowlands especially came to be dominated by dense deciduous forests; hence the importance of some of the ancient tracks across the Downs and other high ground (p. 137). So rapid has been the spread of man, so drastic the change that he and his domestic animals wrought, that little of this original vegetation is left. What we think of as natural scenery is man-made or man-maintained. Our forests are as artificial as our parklands and hedged fields; moorlands and downs are kept in shape by grazing animals. The rough ground about Haytor (p. 27) and the Brecon Beacons (p. 44), even the Highland moors themselves (p. 90), would have different and perhaps more interesting vegetation if the sheep were kept off them for a few years.

The first Britons were small ape-like creatures that infiltrated along the rivers from eastern Europe during a warm spell half a million years ago. We know little of them – only that they used fire, shared the forest with lions, jaguars and bears, and hunted with crude weapons chipped from flints. Closer to ourselves was Neanderthal Man, who arrived in Britain perhaps a quarter of a million years ago. We know him from fragments of bone found among Thames gravels at Swanscombe. Bigger than his predecessors, he lived on more open ground and chipped finer, more specialized tools. Cro-Magnon man, closer still to our own stock, moved across France to Britain some thirty thousand years ago. Elegant flint knives and delicate scrapers were his hallmark; it was his descendants who, in France about fifteen thousand years ago, produced the cave art of Lascaux and La Gravette. Later descendants brought farming to Britain, and dug the shafts of Grime's Graves (p. 122) some five thousand years ago.

Once Britain became an island her shores – visible in fine weather from mainland Europe – began to attract waves of settlers. They crossed in coracles, long-boats and galleys, bringing domestic animals and evidence of their culture – pottery, beads, bronze-ware and ultimately iron. Many were land-hungry farmers, tired of scraping a living on the fringes of continental Europe; those from the north would be tempted by Britain's unoccupied low ground and mild maritime climate. It was Bronze Age man who created the stone circle at Avebury (p. 19) and later Stonehenge, and Iron Age farmers who dug the fort above the White Horse at Uffington (p. 137). When the Romans invaded and took charge the population of Britain numbered about half to three-quarters of a million, made up of several heterogeneous stocks of varying European origin that occupied different zones and kept very much to themselves. After the Romans came Irish invaders from the west, and Angles, Saxons, Jutes, Danes and Norwegians from the east and north, each culture keeping to its own local region and fighting off the neighbours. By the time of the Norman invasion and the Domesday survey of 1086 the British population had doubled. By the end of the fourteenth century it had doubled again; huge areas of the native forest had been cleared or penetrated by small settlements, and Britain was a collection of villages, scattered hamlets and small fortified towns, many of them already supporting splendid churches.

In 1707, when Scotland united with England and Wales under a single crown, there were about seven million Britons. Just less than a century later, at the first national census of 1801, there were ten and a half millions. By this time most of the forest had gone – burnt for domestic heating, iron-working, or simply to clear the land – and most of the population were involved in agriculture. Many tended the flocks of sheep whose meat was the staple diet of those who could afford it, and whose wool brought wealth into Britain from overseas. Now began the changes that converted Britain from an agricultural to a manufacturing society and altered the face of the countryside irrevocably. The Industrial Revolution had already begun close to Ironbridge and at other centres. Mines and quarries developed, roads, canals and railways spread a network of communications, and the population grew at an unprecedented rate, turning villages into towns and towns into ugly, overcrowded cities. By 1821 there were over twenty million Britons, by 1851 over thirty million, and the mass migration of workers from countryside to town was well under way.

Each of these phases of human development and expansion left its mark on Britain, and many of the marks can be seen in the photographs of *Britain from the Air*. Forts, Roman settlements, Norman castles large and small (pp. 144, 148), and Britain's treasury of cathedrals and country houses are among the obvious ones. But almost every picture in this book repays detailed study, perhaps with a reading lens and map. A good road map will do, but far better is a 1:50,000 Ordnance Survey map oriented to match the photograph.

With these you can pick out the finer details – the Roman road that crosses the Brecon Beacons, for example, or the delightful Georgian houses of Bath and Great Malvern (pp. 37 and 41). Close scrutiny will help to reveal the splendid hotch-potch of architectural styles that on a large scale produces Durham (p. 103), Caernarvon (p. 55) and Tewkesbury (p. 40), and on a smaller scale gives us Wivenhoe (p. 129), Aldeburgh (p. 126) and Tenby (p. 48). The crowds at Henley and Donington Park (pp. 139 and 118) are well worth a closer look, and towns like Canterbury, Leicester and Dumfries (pp. 145, 120, 80) make much better sense on the ground, once you have studied them from the air. Look closely, too, at the extraordinary detail of Exeter's wedding-cake cathedral (p. 26) and the curious magic of Waddesdon (p. 150) and Fountains Abbey (p. 105).

But the woods are beautiful as well as the trees. I hope the patterns of these pictures will please just as much as the detail, and help to give everyone a new appreciation of this strangely beautiful country of Britain.

ACKNOWLEDGEMENTS

This book is a cooperative effort involving many helpers. I thank Wilfred Brooker (Managing Director) and Dennis Smith, Peter O'Connell and Christopher Allen of Aerofilms Ltd, for constant help and advice in sorting through the photographic archives. Many people with special knowledge have helped, including P. R. Quarrie (Eton College), David Cotton and Nigel Roome (University of Bradford), David Worth, Joyce Chester, Ken Davies, Jenny Barling, Steve Cox, Michael Mellor, J. R. Guy and A. Boothroyd (Sheffield City Council), and information officers in the British Steel Corporation, British Waterways, the Central Electricity Generating Board, the National Coal Board and British Leyland. Within Weidenfeld & Nicolson it has been a pleasure to work with Russell Ash, who devised the book, Lucy Shankleman (Editor), Julia Brown (Picture Editor), Cathy Ellis (Picture Assistant) and Joyce Chester (Designer). Ann Stonehouse was my assistant in research and preparation of the manuscript.

Beachy Head, East Sussex

A mariners' milestone in the English Channel, Beachy Head is unmistakable from air or sea – 160 metres (520 feet) of sheer chalk cliff that rises above the mists like a vast spread of sails. The lighthouse – you may just be able to see it down on the left – is only 40 metres (130 feet) high, but its 250,000 candlepower beam and noisy foghorn make its presence known when the Head is completely shrouded. Beachy Head stands at the eastern end of a long line of rising cliffs – over eight kilometres (five miles) of them, including the Seven Sisters – that form a rolling, scalloped edge to the South Downs. Between them they make up Britain's longest stretch of chalk cliffs. In stormy weather heaving seas lash the foot of the cliffs and throw spray well inland. The cliff tops, green with turf and bracken, and criss-crossed by sheep-tracks, provide some of the freshest fresh air in Britain. A few Iron Age stalwarts settled along the cliffs, but the sensible folk who followed built their villages in the valleys behind, nestling warmly among the whale-backs of the Downs.

Glyndebourne, East Sussex

Sussex is famous for its chalk downs and sheep. Here, near the village of Glynde, the heartland of the South Downs rises to more than 200 metres (650 feet), then rolls gently in a series of undulations toward the long east-west Vale of Sussex. Just a stone's-throw along the road from Glynde lived John Ellman, the eighteenth-century stockbreeder who first produced the black-faced, finely-fleeced Southdown sheep. But Sussex – at least this part of Sussex – is famous for its music too. This is Glyndebourne, formerly a pleasant but unremarkable Tudor manor house, now an opera centre of world renown. John Christie, the science teacher who inherited Glyndebourne, loved all music and Mozart's in part-icular; so did his wife Audrey, an accomplished operatic singer. In 1934 they turned over their home to music, building on a new opera house and all that goes with it. Glyndebourne is not the grandest of opera houses, but it must surely be the most elegant, in the most idyllic setting. The season runs from May to August.

Rottingdean, East Sussex

Chalk cliffs continue westward along the Sussex coast, lower but still commanding, and cut by deans – sheltered, forested, stream-eroded valleys with long histories of human settlement. Rottingdean stands in just such a valley. The original settlers probably valued it for its shelter and access to the sea. There was never much of a harbour, but early fishermen hauled up their boats at high tide, across the reef and into the creeks. The red-tiled church (top right of picture), built in Norman times some distance from the sea, served a small but well-to-do farming community. As its fine houses of Georgian and earlier times clearly show, Rottingdean has prospered quietly over the centuries. Edwardian artists and writers enjoyed the remoteness and village atmosphere, though Rudyard Kipling became a tourist attraction and had to leave. Neighbouring Brighton drew off the crowds, and the rash of interwar building that gave rise to Saltdean and Peacehaven left only a few villas and bungalows in Rottingdean. Today it is still a prosperous backwater, just right for those who like a quiet life. While visitors come by coach to see its famous toy museum and Kipling relics, holiday recluses cluster in the blocks of flats that so ruthlessly upstage one another on the sea front.

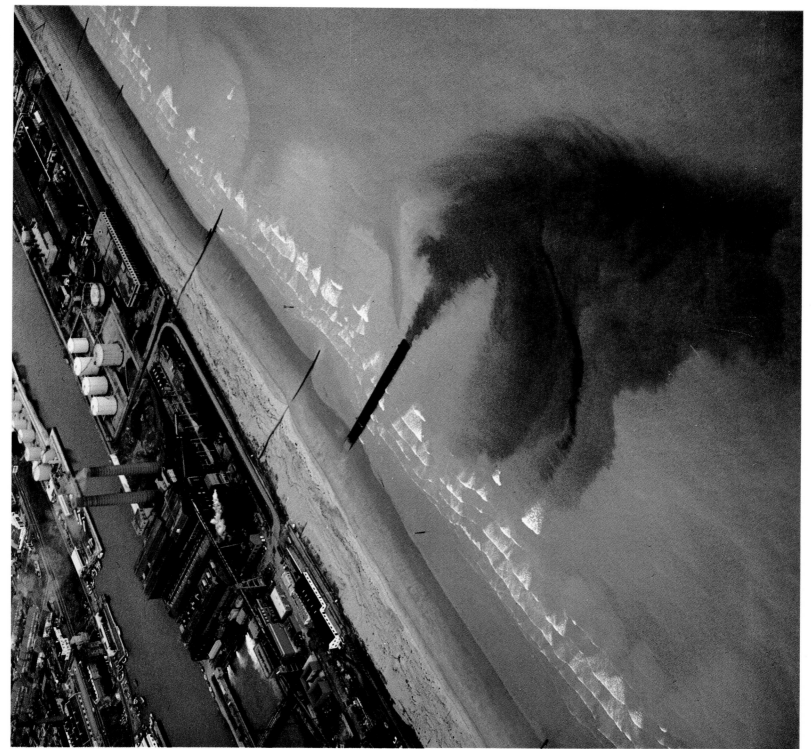

Shoreham and Portslade, West Sussex

At Shoreham-by-Sea (below, foreground) and Portslade (background and right) massive shingle banks that form along the coast divert the River Adur eastward. The result – a fine natural harbour and yacht basin more than five kilometres (three miles) long. Once the haunt of seabirds, Shoreham is now a busy port where coasters and pleasure craft cheerfully get in one another's way. This is not a gentle coast. The sea beats constantly against the outer bank and strong currents tend to drift sand and shingle eastward; hence the long wooden groynes, that point accusingly at the sea and try to bring it to order. There are good beaches, mostly pebbled, but sandy in patches and wild enough for anyone in winter. Hardy people build sand-castles and swim off the groynes at Portslade, as though this were still an undeveloped area. However, the huge power station, with its smokestacks and effluent outfall, and the drab industrial complex nearby, make it clear that this area means business. There are pleasures aplenty for those who want them, just a few kilometres up the coast at Brighton and Hove.

Portsmouth, Hampshire

Portsmouth, Langstone and Chichester Harbours are splendid, sheltered inlets on the Hampshire coast, lying between Spithead and Selsey Bill, and separated by Portsea and Hayling Islands. Of the three it was Portsmouth that developed and industrialized, becoming Britain's largest and most important naval base in the south. Richard Coeur de Lion began it all in 1194, by founding a small settlement on the west flank of Portsea Island, under the protection of Porchester Castle. (The castle's walls can just be seen at the back of the harbour, on the right.) So began Portsmouth town, which with its dockyards, naval establishments, factories and suburbs, has gradually spread to cover most of the island. A naval base and commercial port for more than 500 years, Portsmouth has been known to generations of seamen as Pompey. Its harbour, lined with mudbanks, has never been popular with navigators, but its citizens and the Navy understand each other and get on well together. Though the battleships have gone, Pompey survives; there are plenty of smaller grey ships to keep the naval traditions going, and the harbour fills with pleasure craft on windy summer days. Southsea (occupying the foreground of this picture) is a pleasant holiday resort, much favoured by sailors home from the sea. Its castle dates from the sixteenth century, its fortress from the mid-nineteenth century, when Britain armed to protect itself once again from the perfidious French. There is a line of older forts on the mainland behind the harbour, along the chalky ridge of Portsdown. Neighbouring Gosport and Alverstoke lie to the west of the harbour mouth.

Hamble, Hampshire

Hamble stands on Southampton Water at the mouth of the Hamble river. A natural haven, for centuries it has provided anchorage, fresh water and a run-ashore for mariners. Saxons and Danes knew it well, and it probably saw its share of smuggling – perhaps it still does – from boats big enough to brave the Channel and bring home the brandy from France. Today it is still a haven, but now the small ships are pleasure craft. Hamble offers moorings, marinas, repair yards, chandlery, and comfort ashore for yachtsmen of all kinds in caravans, chalets and pubs. For those who prefer to stay ashore it provides spectacle; a hundred small boats under sail are a pretty sight, and there is always the chance that a few will turn over, to the huge delight of the rest.

Osborne House, Isle of Wight

Queen Victoria visited the Isle of Wight several times in her youth. She found it much to her taste, and decided to buy a small estate there – a private retreat for herself and her growing family to be paid for from her own pocket. After some haggling, she bought the Osborne estate of 400 hectares (1,000 acres) complete with residence for £26,000, taking possession in April 1845. As the original house was too small, her consort Prince Albert designed a bigger one; his many gifts included a flair for architecture and a healthy disregard for establishment taste. The Osborne setting reminded Albert of the Bay of Naples, so he designed an Italianate villa. He was helped by Thomas Cubitt, whose work in a similar vein was already to be seen – as indeed it still is – on the best residential areas of Kensington. Furnishings and gardens were designed to match. There is a splendidly ornate billiard table, and a somewhat anatomical collection of marble arms, legs, and hands, modelled from the royal children as they grew up. Osborne House seems to have been a happy home for Victoria, Albert and their family, giving them the peace they sought after the bustle of London. The children even had an authentic Swiss cottage of their own to play in. There were woods, fields and a beach to divert them, and resident nightingales that sang when Albert whistled. Victoria spent much of her retirement here, and died at Osborne in 1901. If today it looks institutional, that may be because Albert chose a practical, uncluttered style of building that institution designers favour. About a kilometre from East Cowes (background), Osborne House is now a convalescent home. The state rooms are open to the public.

The Needles, Isle of Wight

To navigators the Needles are a line of sharp-ridged rocks that extend westward from the Isle of Wight, marking the end of the Solent. Wise ones give them a wide berth, for they continue westward beyond the lighthouse as a line of reefs; the invisible needles below the surf are just as dangerous as the ones you can see. Cross winds, tidal surges and currents make this a tricky bit of coast at the best of times and a seaman's nightmare at the worst. To geologists, the Needles are part of the fold system that crumpled the Alps, the Pyrenees, and the Himalaya some 30 million years ago and spread across Europe as far as southern Britain. By then their energy was almost spent, but to them we owe the basin-shape of the Weald, the South Downs, the chalky ridge behind Portsmouth Harbour, and the long, narrow ridge, almost parallel to Portsdown, that forms the east-west axis of the Isle of Wight. Called Tennyson Down, the ridge runs straight up from the Needles toward Easton and Freshwater Bay; there is a monument to the poet Lord Tennyson half way along it. The chalk continues right across the island, emerging at the eastern end as Culver Cliff. Its southern flank rests on older, softer strata – the sandstones and clays that alternate along the island's south shore. Against its northern flank lap the much younger sandstones of Alum Bay, banded in bright colours from pink to rusty brown. You can buy glass jars of coloured sands from the kiosk on the cliff-top.

Salisbury, Wiltshire

Salisbury, one of England's earliest New Towns, was established in 1220 to replace the cathedral town of Sarum a few kilometres to the north. Old Sarum proved unsatisfactory because of its erratic water supply: new Salisbury stands where lesser rivers join the Avon, so should never run short of water. Cathedral and town were founded together. Built in less than 40 years in a single style (now called Early English), Salisbury Cathedral is a jewel; every part of it matches every other part and a walled close provides the perfect setting. The spire, added in 1334, rises over 120 metres (404 feet) and is the tallest in Britain. The town has grown, but the simple grid-pattern of thirteenth-century New Sarum can still be seen beyond the cathedral, and a ring road diverts much of the heavy traffic away to the east.

Avebury Rings, Wiltshire

The Downs of central Wiltshire were well-populated during the Neolithic and Bronze Ages by folk who were not afraid of re-arranging the countryside substantially to meet their own needs. Stonehenge on Salisbury Plain, three to four thousand years old, is their most famous monument. Avebury may be slightly older; less compact, it is harder to appreciate on the ground, but shows up well from the air. The outer bank of chalk rubble has a diameter of over 420 metres (1,400 feet) and stands five to six metres (15–20 feet) high. It was probably higher originally. The ditch inside, from which it was dug, was about ten metres (30 feet) deep. Within stands a ring of sarsens – slabs of unhewn sandstone, set upright in the chalk. There were originally about 100 of them, but well over half have been broken up and used for walling in the village and surrounding farms. Inside the main circle were lesser sarsen rings, possibly older. What was it all about? Nobody knows. Avebury stands at a meeting-place of ancient trackways across the Downs. It may have been a sacred place, and also a gathering-ground where sheep and cattle could be herded safely – perhaps while their Bronze Age owners traded insults with rude Neolithics across the ditch. Like Stonehenge, and every other monument of its kind, it took a lot of putting together.

Stourhead, Wiltshire

In 1718, four years into the reign of George 1, the London banker Henry Hoare built a Palladian mansion on an estate near Stourton, in the south-western corner of Wiltshire. Wealth, a taste for things classical and a flair for gardening seem to have been handed on in equal parts to the generations succeeding him. The gardens, enhanced in 1741 by the creation of a large lake, were landscaped by the second Henry Hoare (son of the founder) and decorated in the Classical style. Henry had lost his wife and three of his children in tragic succession, and creating a garden absorbed most of his energies for almost 40 years. Buildings scattered about the lake included a Temple of Flora (visible in this picture across the lake), a Temple of Apollo, and a Pantheon. Several Gothic follies and Bristol's old market cross were added by way of variety. There is also a curious three-sided tower 50 metres (160 feet) high that commemorates King Alfred's victory over the Danes in 879. Henry Hoare the younger and his successors also planted many fine trees and shrubs, both native and exotic. Meanwhile the house filled gradually with British and Italian paintings, sculpture, porcelain and furniture. Stourhead and its gardens, with their gentle, inspired dottiness, were handed over to the National Trust in 1947; both are well worth a visit.

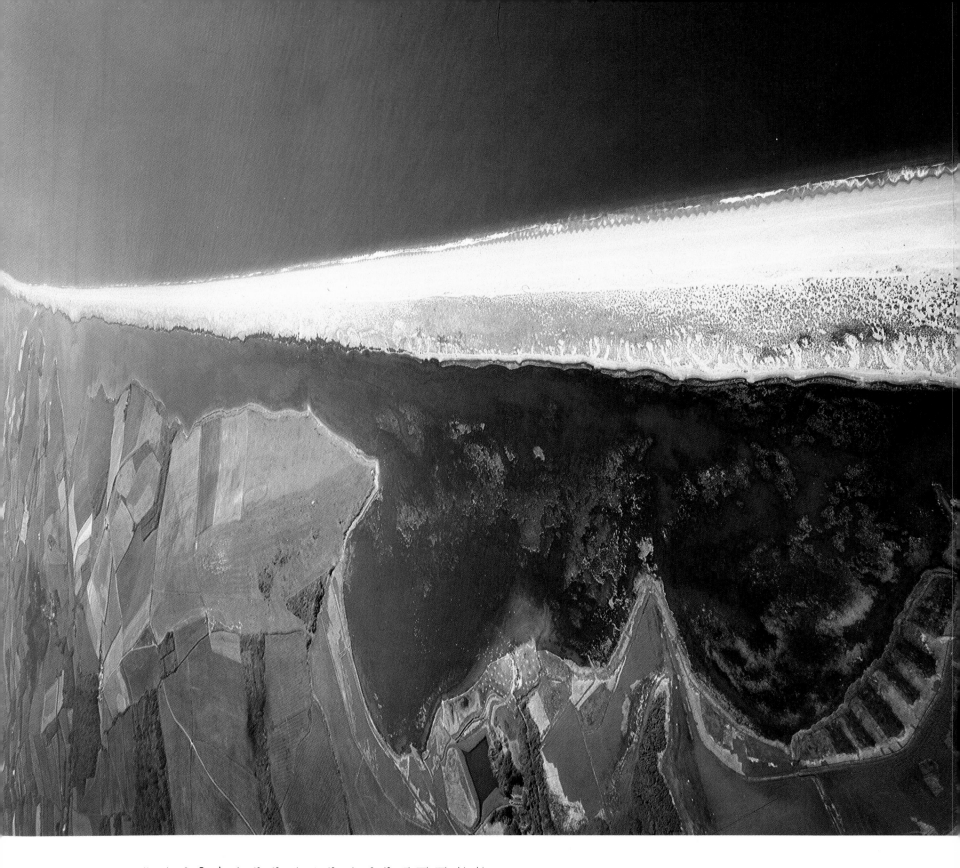

Chesil Beach, Dorset

Much of the eastern end of Lyme Bay is edged with a steep, narrow, pebble beach – almost 30 kilometres (18 miles) of it from Burton Bradstock to the limestone island of Portland. From Abbotsbury eastward the beach is cut off from its hinterland by East and West Fleet, shallow lagoons fed by coastal streams. So the last 20 kilometres (12 miles) or more form this strange breakwater, an isolated bank of pebbles running from northwest to south-east in a gentle, elegant curve. The pebbles are graded – fist-sized at the Portland end, mere golf-balls at Abbotsbury – and constantly re-sorted by storms and wave action. Chesil Beach is no place to be in a storm. The waves break high and there are reports of small ships being lifted right over and dumped in The Fleet – a problem for skippers, for there is no way out. The Fleet, shallow and saline, provides good feeding for the swans that gather in their hundreds in winter. Several dozen can be seen here, close to their traditional breeding ground near Abbotsbury. They are said to have been encouraged there by the Benedictine monks who once lived at Abbotsbury. My guess is that the swans were there first and the monks knew a good thing when they saw one.

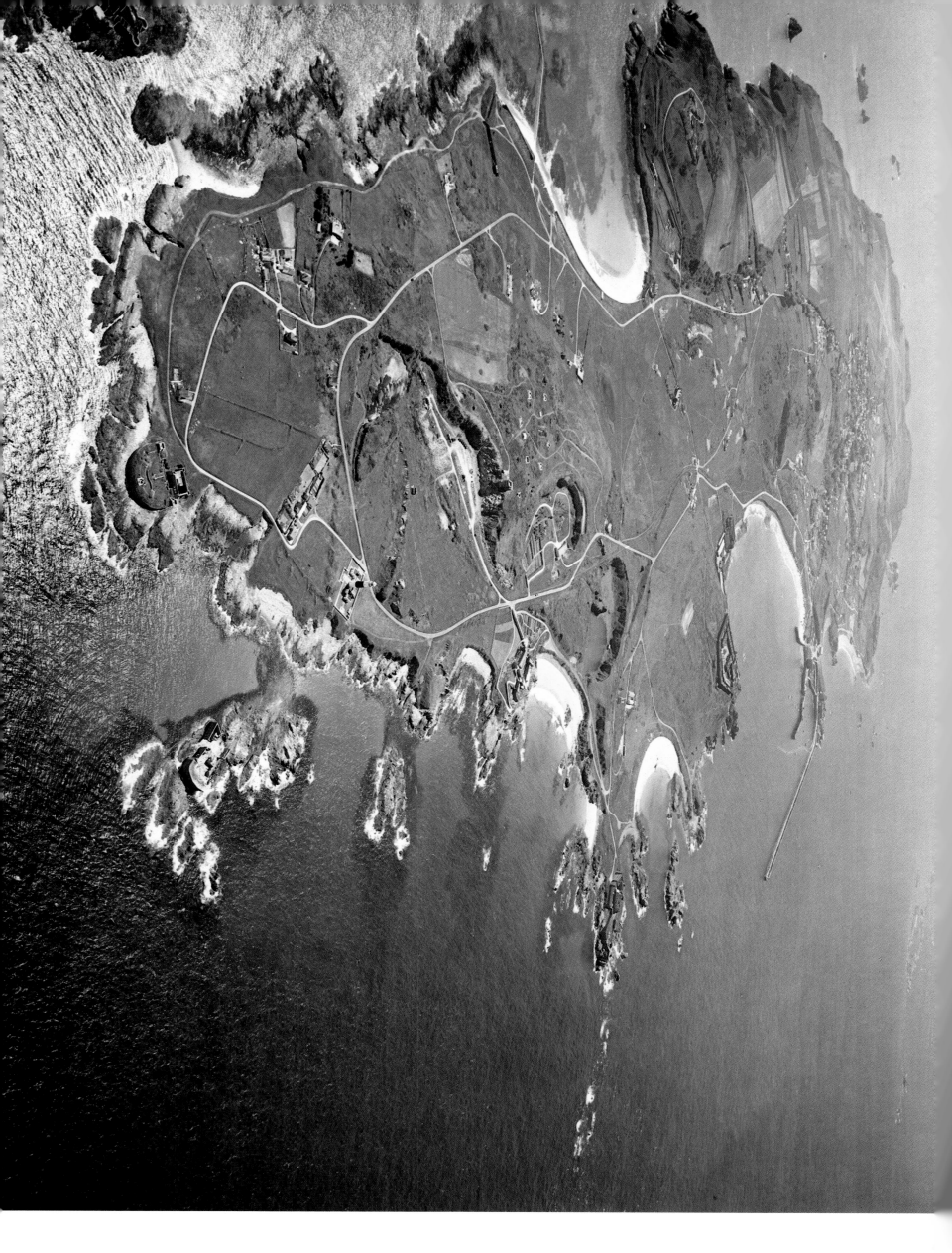

Alderney, Channel Islands

The Romans called it Riduna, the French call it Aurigny; to the British it is Alderney and, like most of the Channel Islands, a British Crown Dependency. Despite their position only a few kilometres from the coast of France, the Channel Islands have been linked to Britain since William the Conqueror's time – they were part of his Duchy of Normandy. Under the Crown they are to a large extent self-governing; Alderney's 1,700 residents are included in the Bailiwick of Guernsey, but have their own nine-member parliament to settle local affairs. Seen here from the east, Alderney is an irregular green table tilted slightly towards us. In the foreground ancient sedimentary rocks have been quarried for building stone; beyond the two bays harder granites rise to form high cliffs in the south and west. St Anne's, the main settlement, overlooks the wide, sweeping bay of Braye Harbour, with its protective mole. Almost every corner and off-lying islet was fortified, by the British against possible French incursions during the nineteenth century.

Jersey, Channel Islands

Tucked well into the French coast and over 150 kilometres (nearly 100 miles) from Britain, Jersey is the largest and most French of all the Channel Islands. It is also the most heavily populated, with 70,000 residents seeking their livelihood on fewer than 120 square kilometres (47 square miles) of none too promising island. But Jerseymen (and women) seem always to have kept ahead. In the old days they were pirates and colonists, deep-sea fishermen and soldiers of fortune – and always dedicated farmers who improved their poor island soils by what would today be called organic husbandry. Jersey's forte was and still is dairy farming, based exclusively on its cream-coloured, glamorous, but intensely practical short-horn cattle. But wherever the soils allow, crops are important too, for Jersey is always a few weeeks ahead of Britain climatically and can catch the early markets. This cherished corner south-east of St Helier shows how Jersey's green-fingered community makes use of its natural advantages. Early potatoes, tomatoes, greens and flowers are the chief money-spinners, but the annual crop of tourists pays best of all.

Salcombe, Devon

Parts of Britain are slowly disappearing beneath the sea – perhaps under the weight of population or the national debt. Here in south Devon it is all to the good, because the drowned river valleys make splendid harbours. You have to watch yourself and your boat, for there is often a sandbar across the mouth and the tide can go out a long way and leave you stranded for hours. But Salcombe is not a bad place to be stranded. The beaches are sandy, the waters warm in summer, and stranded folk with money to spend are well looked after ashore. The village grew up from practically nothing. In the mid-nineteenth century there were two scruffy inns and the bones of an old castle on the point, but very little else. It began with ship-building. Salcombe-built schooners sailed the south coast of Britain and crossed regularly to the Mediterranean for oranges and lemons. Today Salcombe caters mainly for tourists ashore and yachtsmen afloat, while oranges and lemons manage to grow – perhaps to their own surprise as much as anyone else's – among other exotic trees in the bungalow gardens.

Brixham, Devon

Brixham was little more than a fishing village when William of Orange landed here in 1688, guttural but well-intentioned toward his new kingdom. 'I am here for your goot – for all of your goots', he is said to have said, before starting out for London. Brixham's good times began in the early nineteenth century when local enterprise built the harbour mole, and local fishermen invented both the trawl net and the sturdy, sail-powered Brixham trawler to tow it over the sea bed. Brixham men took fish to London and stayed to trawl the Thames. They found their way up to East Anglia and Yorkshire, teaching the locals the new craft in broad Devon burr. Today Brixham is part of the south coast complex of towns centred on Tor Bay. While Torquay and Paignton cater self-consciously for the tourists and retired folk, Brixham stays primarily a fishing port. The inner harbour berths a replica of the *Golden Hind* but there are modern trawlers off-loading down at the fish-quay.

Exeter, Devon

Capital of Devon and almost central to it, Exeter stands at the point where the River Exe broadens to form an estuary. Though 15 kilometres (nine miles) from the coast it has a sea-going air about it, for Exeter has long been a port, and a reasonably prosperous one despite many ups and downs. It began as the Roman Isca Dunnoniorum. The Saxon invaders made it their local capital, and the Danes found it worth sacking several times – even living in it for three years. William of Normandy had to besiege Exeter for over a fortnight before it finally accepted him in 1068. A sixteenth-century Countess of Devonshire built a weir across the river to spoil its chances as a port; Exeter countered by building a ship canal and taking her to court. The cathedral was started before the Norman conquest and grew under William's patronage. However, in the thirteenth century it was partly dismantled and rebuilt, so it ends up with twin Norman towers on the transepts and just about everything else in elaborate English Decorated style. Like others of its kind, Exeter Cathedral benefits from its setting of lawns and Georgian houses. The city, too, has a wealth of good architecture, dating mostly from its heyday in the eighteenth and early nineteenth centuries, and new buildings are still going up. Much of its prosperity came from serge, a tough west-country fabric that used both long-staple and short-staple Devonshire wools. The weaving took place in many centres, but Exeter provided the main export outlet.

Haytor, Dartmoor, Devon

Dartmoor is the top of a huge granite mushroom that long ago forced itself, as a white-hot liquid, through all but the uppermost layers of the earth's crust. There it cooled and solidified. Because of the layers of rock still above, the granite cooled slowly, producing a hard, resistant rock of large, interlocking crystals. Now erosion has worn the surface strata away, leaving a granite dome thinly covered in acid soils. With similar mushrooms in the southwest, Dartmoor provides some of our wildest and most spectacular scenery. Though a large area of it is gazetted a National Park, not all is open to the public. Some is privately owned, some farmed, some set aside for military training, and one small area (curiously a major tourist attraction) is devoted to Her Majesty's Prison and its unlovely surroundings at Princetown. Sixteen kilometres (ten miles) to the east of Princetown is a wilder, rougher area of Dartmoor, threaded with quarry roads. Here we find Haytor, one of many granite crags that rise above their surroundings and afford matchless views for those who get to the top in fine weather. There is usually an easy way up for walkers, but these crags of hard rock are a mecca for climbers too; the photographer has caught both in his picture.

East and West Looe, Cornwall

The Looe and West Looe Rivers join just behind the bridge, which in turn links the paired towns of East and West Looe. The two face each other across their narrow estuary, similar but different like Darby and Joan. Though joined by a bridge for many centuries, they remained separate communities until 1883. East Looe is the larger partner, with a sixteenth-century guildhall, a seventeenth-century inn, and a business-like water-front lined with old warehouses. Whatever its present role, East Looe worked long and hard at fishing, mining and a host of other activities for many centuries. West Looe is smaller, gentler and prettier – more of a residential suburb, though it too has its quay and evidence of an industrial past. Above the towns on either side rise the boarding houses and rented accommodation that tell of the present, for both East and West Looe are geared up for the holiday trade. East Looe has the fine sandy beach, West Looe the rocks and cliffs. Both have the good sense to cater for the tourists who pour in to see them each year. With their beauty and quaintness, their tea-shops and craft-shops, the Looes have plenty to offer. Less heroic than fishing? Less productive than mining? But the mines are dead, the fishing is dead, and the tourists are queuing to come in. Either way it's hard work for the people of East and West Looe.

Carluddon, near St Austell, Cornwall

Industry has created strange landscapes up and down Britain and here is one of the strangest. The product is kaolin or China clay, formed from the breakdown of feldspars, which are one of the constituents of granite. Kaolin has a hundred industrial uses, for example in paper-making, and the porcelain, cosmetics, paint and rubber industries. There are only a few places in the world where it occurs in large quantities, and Cornwall, just above St Austell, is one of the most important. Dug from open pits and washed to refine it, kaolin is bagged, or sent down the coast in bulk. It leaves behind huge heaps of tailings and deep pits filled with ice-blue water – a lunar landscape that now extends from St Austell to Bugle, and from Fraddon to St Dennis, Hensbarrow and Luxulyan. Kaolin is a fine white powder that gets everywhere. On dry, windy days it rises in clouds above the workings; on wet days it washes down to a fine mud that turns the rivers and even the sea milky. Some of the open-cast pits that yield kaolin have also in their time yielded ores of tin and copper, and St Austell has reaped benefit from all of them.

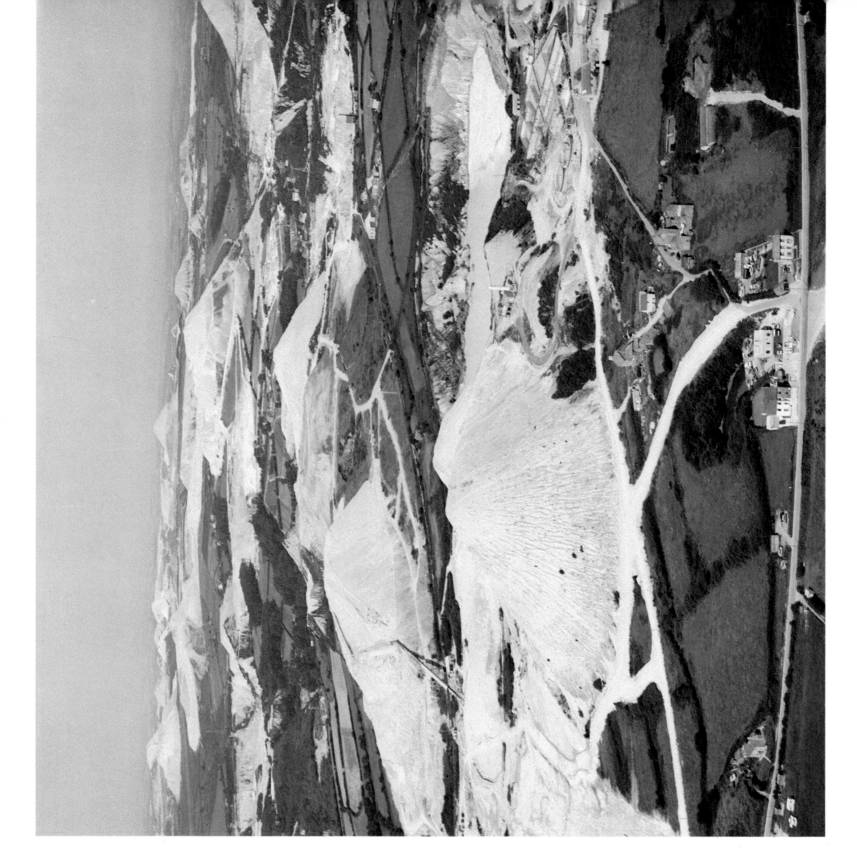

St Ives, Cornwall

St Ives stands on the mainland and spreads over a narrow isthmus with broad, sandy beaches on either side. The west is exposed, with fine surfing for those who like it; to the east is a sheltered bay, with a granite mole built by Smeaton, who also built the first Eddystone lighthouse at the other end of Cornwall. Settlement began with a sixth-century chapel to a Cornish saint, and a fishing and mining community developed. Built sturdy against the south-westerly gales, isolated by distance and sheer remoteness from the rest of the country, it has made its own way through history. St Ives sheltered Perkin Warbeck and favoured him against King Henry VII in 1497, and supported Parliament in a mainly Royalist Cornwall during the Civil War. John Wesley was well received – but so in their turn were the artists, including Whistler and Sickert, who brought a touch of Bohemia to strait-laced St Ives in the 1890s. Visitors from outside became welcome when the small-boat pilchard fishing failed. Now St Ives, still famous for its artists, is a holiday resort and truly delightful when the sun shines.

St Michael's Mount, Cornwall

At the back of Mount's Bay, just over a kilometre from the coast, stands an island mound of silvery granite, topped by a church and a fortified house. At low tide a causeway connects it to the mainland. There are the ruins of a medieval watchtower and fortifications, and much older buildings and artefacts too, for St Michael's Mount has been occupied continuously for well over 1,000 years. The first dwelling was probably a hermit's cell. French monks came over to found a small monastery in 1135. Their church fell in a severe earthquake 140 years later, and the present one, dating from the fourteenth century, was built to replace it. St Michael's Mount, at the gateway to the Channel, has had a chequered history. Garrisoned, fought over, occupied by pirates and rebels of all kinds, this tiny island with its aura of sanctity seems always to have generated violence, even when the rest of the country was at peace. Now it can relax; like Marazion, that faces it on the mainland, it is just another holiday diversion on a peculiarly attractive length of coast.

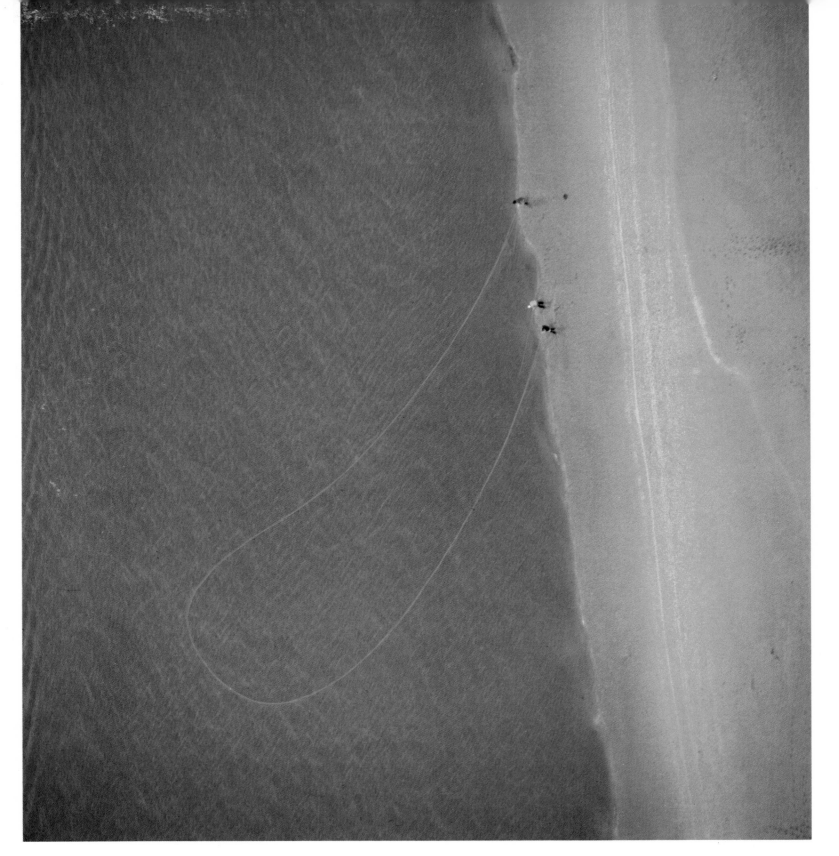

Red River, Godrevy, Cornwall

They call it the Red River, though it is only an overgrown stream that enters the sea just across the bay from St Ives. It starts from a source high on the moors beyond Bolenowe Crofts, over toward Nine Maidens Downs, and flows north by Treskillard and Brea. Taking a turn around Camborne it runs by disused mines and quarry tailings, picking up what it must from the workings. At Roscroggan it shifts westward past the tin works. Close to Coombe it enters the valley that takes it to Ashill and on to Nancemellin, where it picks up its last major tributary. By the time it is flowing past Godrevy Towans the Red River is crimson, pouring into the sea like blood from an artery, staining the beach and tinting the surf as it goes. Needless to say, its mineral content is high; tin and other metals have been recovered from it. Perhaps one day someone will tell somebody else to get it cleaned up, pursuant to some act or other, and be quick about it. Meanwhile the Red River is just another touch of colour in a colourful corner of Britain.

Appledore, Devon

A timeless picture that could have been taken any day, anywhere in the world. They might be Chinese, Polynesians or Aleuts. They could be in Sri Lanka, the Red Sea or the Sea of Galilee, and their catch might be any of a thousand kinds of fish that tempt fate by feeding inshore. In fact these fishermen are British, as far as we know, fishing for whatever they can catch with a seine net off a north Devonshire sandspit.

Clevedon, Avon

Far up the Severn Estuary, washed by a muddy sea, stands a charming Victorian seaside resort. Built mainly by the enterprise of the Elton family, Clevedon retains an atmosphere that few other resorts have managed to hold – 'the most character, the widest diversity of scenery, the fewest really hideous buildings ...' wrote John Betjeman, and a great deal more in its favour as well. Its houses, were small, comfortable villas, its clientele probably the carriage trade from Bristol and Clifton, for this was their closest resort. Clevedon gave them the sea, presentable, if a little murky, within an easy morning's drive. Lesser folk took the light railway from Portishead. The pier, opened in 1869, set a seal of perfection on an already near-perfect summer resort. Whatever happened to it? About a century after the pier was built, somebody decided it needed checking. In the process it got broken. Now there is a Save Clevedon Pier appeal to put it together again.

Severn Bridge, Avon

Opened in 1966, the Severn Bridge carries the M4 motorway across the river from Aust Cliff in Avon (left) to Beachley in Gloucestershire. The Severn is 1,600 metres (one mile) wide at this point, but the span – the distance between towers – is what counts with suspension bridges. This has a span of 988 metres (3,200 feet), about 20 metres (65 feet) less than the Forth Road Bridge; both are tiddlers compared with the new Humber Bridge which spans over 1,400 metres (4,600 feet). Wind is the great enemy of suspension bridges, and the Severn Bridge included new features of design to reduce its effects. The decking that carries the roadway is a box girder only three metres (ten feet) deep, shaped like an aircraft wing to reduce wind eddies. The suspender cables supporting the deck are rigged in pairs, splaying outward at the bottom to damp down wind-induced oscillation. Crossing in a strong wind can still be quite an experience, but like any other good engineering job, the Severn Suspension Bridge breeds confidence by simply looking right. It is a beautiful bridge in an attractive setting, and a useful unit in Britain's motorway system.

Clifton Gorge, Bristol, Avon

Britain has several rivers called Avon, and quite a few Afons, Afons and other variants – not surprisingly, for they are all based on the Celtic word for 'river'. No other Avon has cut quite so spectacular a channel for itself as the Lower or Bristol Avon, that starts in the south-eastern Cotswolds not far from Malmesbury, and flows in a wide circle through Chippenham, Melksham, Bradford-on-Avon and Bath. By the time it passes through Bristol it has gained several tributaries. Here at Clifton, on the southern outskirts of Bristol, it pours sluggishly into the steep-sided gorge it has carved for itself through a low limestone ridge. Ships coming into Bristol had to pass through the gorge – no easy task under sail, and a disadvantage that has handicapped Bristol through the centuries. Clifton developed as a residential suburb from the late eighteenth century onward, its Georgian and Victorian terraces rising high above the murk of the city. The suspension bridge, designed by Brunel and started in 1836, took 28 years to finish. Money ran out, and the bridge was eventually completed with second-hand chains from Hungerford foot-bridge, an earlier creation of Brunel's that was being demolished. Two hundred metres (650 feet) long, it hangs 75 metres (250 feet) over the river at high water, linking Clifton with Leigh Woods, Portishead, and the seaside resort of Clevedon.

Bath, Avon

Between Bradford and Bristol the Lower Avon swings northward and then turns sharply west, cutting through limestone and forming a terraced amphitheatre. Warm springs in the hillsides attracted the Romans, who built their settlement of Aquae Sulis on the bend of the river. Their bath-house can still be visited in the centre of Bath, the city that grew up around it. The Bath of today is centred on a delightful Georgian township of planned terraces, crescents and squares, dating from around 1730. Its main architects were a team of father and son, both called John Wood, who took over a rambling, overgrown medieval village and turned it into a fashionable spa. Their backers were the Dukes of Chandos, who owned the land, and Ralph Allen, a wealthy quarry-owner. Their style was Palladian, and their building material a warm, honey-brown oolitic limestone from Allen's quarries at Combe Down, just south of the city. Robert Adam contributed designs (notably the enclosed Pulteney Bridge across the Avon), and Beau Nash set a spanking pace for social life in the new town. Bath fell into a decline during the nineteenth century, which is probably as well; if it had stayed wealthy, progressive folk would have modernized their Georgian inheritance out of existence. Now it is there for us all to enjoy – the raffish, old-fashioned heart of a bustling modern city.

Highgrove, near Tetbury, Gloucestershire

Castles and palaces are all very fine, but for comfortable, well-designed houses-for-living, small British country mansions are hard to beat. From Tudor times onward, prosperous citizens who had made their capital retired to the country and built. Bankers and city men, manufacturers, physicians, officers retiring with prize money or gratuities – they all looked forward to their country house, with its farm for fresh produce, its acres for shooting, and its gardens for designing, replanting and growing. They had to be sizeable family houses, with room for the children, unmarried sisters, aged parents and aunts, and a big staff to keep things in order. Some of the best were simple and unpretentious, with well-

proportioned rooms and pleasing vistas from every window. Country houses of this kind convert well for modern living, and are still very popular, though among the young it is usually only princes and pop-singers who can afford them. Here is just such a house, in a small estate not far from Stroud, with stabling (suit horse lovers) and kennels, Range-Rover-sized garages, and farm attached; the garden would stand some improvement. But Highgrove is not on the market at present. The people who owned it, with a name well-known in publishing, sold it recently to a young retired naval officer with a name well-known everywhere, who seems set on raising his own family there.

The Duntisbournes, Gloucestershire

The Duntisbournes lie just a few kilometres from Cirencester on the south-eastern flank of the Cotswolds. Duntisbourne means 'Dunt's stream', and there are four settlements that bear the name. Duntisbourne Abbots belonged formerly to the Benedictine abbey at Gloucester; there it is nestling among the trees in the background. How Duntisbourne Leer got its name I cannot discover and hesitate to guess, but it includes the two nearer settlements. Duntisbourne Rouse once belonged to Roger le Rus or 'Red Roger', back in the thirteenth century, and Middle Duntisbourne falls somewhere between them all; both lie to the south, and off this picture. Guidebooks say little of these quiet little places. Main roads and railways have mercifully kept away, though Ermine Street (now the A417) runs close by Duntisbourne Abbots and the Romans had a villa there. Like other remote villages of Britain these days, they may be difficult to live in, and could get more difficult for the young who are bored, the old who are isolated, and those without cars of their own. But strongly built in Cotswold style, stone-walled and well-roofed, these villages have survived plagues, feuds, civil wars, poverty and wealth for hundreds of years. Declining bus services and threats to cut amenities may come and go, but there is every indication that the Duntisbournes – all four of them – will be there to give a guarded, Cotswold account of themselves when the last trump sounds.

Tewkesbury, Gloucestershire

Tewkesbury stands at the junction of two rivers, the Severn and the Upper Avon, and on their joint flood plain. The town (lying mostly to the right of the picture) grew up close to an abbey, whose Norman tower still dominates its skyline. The monks who began it and the citizens who followed were wise enough to build on a ridge. It was a slight one, but just enough to lift them above the level of flood water when the spring rains fell and the rivers backed up – as they have backed up here. The dominant Severn is on the left of the photograph, and the flooded Avon – Shakespeare's Avon – is trying to discharge paler waters into it from the right. The A38 from Worcester to Gloucester crosses on a raised viaduct, with the track of an old railway line behind it. Close to Tewkesbury was fought one of the nastiest battles of the Wars of the Roses, when Margaret of Anjou's Lancastrians were routed in 1471 by the Yorkists under Edward IV. Behind rises Bredon Hill, centrepiece of Housman's sad verses.

Great Malvern, Hereford and Worcester

The Malvern Hills, shared between the old counties of Hereford and Worcester, now form a north-south backbone for the new joint county. Tiny by world standards, they still rise impressively over the plains. Worcestershire Beacon (right foreground) here stands 421 metres (1,380 feet) above sea level, and a good 350 metres (1,150 feet) above the surrounding fields. If the Malverns have a well-used look about them it is really not surprising. Their ancient rocks are all of 600 million years old, and seem to have been standing proud above the landscape for much of that time. The National Trust has taken most of them under its wing. By planting trees and maintaining pathways, it is trying to protect their surface against erosion, the erosion caused when too many pairs of boots walk – however appreciatively – on thin hillside soils. This is the town of Great Malvern, on the north-eastern flank; Little Malvern lies in the distance beyond the dip. Built originally about a Benedictine Priory, Great Malvern retains its superb Priory Church of St Mary and St Michael, glowing with medieval glass. In the eighteenth century it became a spa town, capitalizing on its Malvern Water from mineral springs. It has survived, like many other British towns, quite simply because it is a pleasant place to live in. Musicians like it; there is an annual Malvern Festival, and Sir Edward Elgar – the area's other patron saint – lies buried in Little Malvern.

Bredwardine, Hereford and Worcester

Drifting westward across the Malverns to Hereford, and westward again along the Wye Valley, we cross red sandstone country, and a fine, rusty red everything becomes. Cliffs and crags are red, castle and cowshed walls glow like russet apples. Stream-beds are red as the Hereford cattle that drink from them; so are newly-turned fields and gravelled country lanes. Spring introduces new motifs of pink, white and green as the orchards burst into flower. The buildings – those that belong – take on these colours and glow unashamedly. Here in the village of Bredwardine, in the Wye Valley

close by the Welsh border, stands a russet-red church with a sugar-pink vicarage, both real, and both right for their setting. Indeed, both are famous, for the church, with its Norman nave and slightly skewed chancel, is the one where Francis Kilvert ministered for the two years before his death in 1879. He is buried in the churchyard close by. In the candy-floss vicarage alongside he wrote some of the final pages of his diary – the remarkable diary of a country parson that came to light in 1937 and turned into a best-seller almost a century after his death.

Vale of Ewyas, Powys

The Black Mountains of south-eastern Wales show more clearly than any textbook how glaciers have shaped the scenery. They lie between two rivers, the Wye and the Usk. Hay-on-Wye stands at the north end and Abergavenny at the south. Formed by a dome of ancient sandstone, they were planed to a smooth, rounded surface during an early glacial period some hundreds of thousands of years ago. In a later round of glaciation the moving rivers of ice cut down through the surface, gouging deep, parallel grooves that run roughly north and south, separated from their neighbours by slab-sided sandstone remnants. The tops of the ridges are of uniform height, representing the original domed surface. These sandstones, covered with poor acid soils, support little more than bracken and coarse brown grass. The valley floors 300–400 metres (1,000–1,300 feet) below are green and fertile, well watered by streams and well tended from farms dotted along the valley. Here we drift over the top of Hatterall Hill, which rises to 531 metres (1,740 feet), and look north up the long Vale of Ewyas. You can just see the village of Llanthony, with its ancient priory, where the valley floor broadens. The road follows the river along the centre of the valley, taking the right fork out over Gospel Pass to Hay-on-Wye.

Brecon Beacons, Powys

West of the Black Mountains the Old Red Sandstones, locally harder and more resistant to erosion, produce a more dramatic landscape. Between Brecon and Merthyr Tydfil stands a high dome that the glaciers have carved, not into gentle valleys, but into steep-sided corrie basins with razor-backed ridges between. The highest ridges are the Brecon Beacons, so-called because they can be seen for miles; in the old days beacon fires were lit on them to signal danger or rejoicing. The highest point, closest to us on the right, is Pen y fan at 886 metres (2,900 feet) above sea level. The high point in the centre is Cribin, just 91 metres (300 feet) lower, and the little lakes beyond are the highest of the Neuadd reservoirs. There is a much larger reservoir, Taf Fechan, in the top right corner; the two are joined, and their waters drop southward to slake the industrial thirst of Merthyr Tydfil, just a few kilometres further on. A track that climbs out of the corrie behind Cribin, crosses the ridge and drives a straight line along the slope behind the reservoir (you may just be able to spot it with a lens), is – incredibly enough – the Roman road from Brecon to Merthyr.

Treherbert, Mid Glamorgan

South of the Brecon Beacons, and a surprisingly short step south, wild Wales shifts character abruptly and becomes industrial Wales. Here at Treherbert, less than 25 kilometres (15 miles) from Pen y fan, we have crossed the boundary and are drifting down a valley – perhaps the most famous of all the valleys – towards Cardiff and the industrial heartland. The valleys are furrows in the bed of an ancient, shallow sea that long ago covered South Wales. Deepened by erosion, the furrows give access to coal – a fossil relic of ferny swamps that lined the old sea shore. At Treherbert, high up the valley of the little Rhondda river, pits dug in 1855 exposed the high quality steam coal that was to make the valley famous. Mining spread down the Rhondda as the railway climbed it – Treorchy, Tonypandy and other centres developed, forming a ribbon of mining communities along the valley floor. Hard times came to the Rhondda in the years between the wars when oil replaced coal in steam boilers. But the communities have survived, strengthened by chapel, song, and light industries introduced to diversify the economy.

Cardiff Docks, South Glamorgan

When the flow of coal and iron from the valleys began in the early nineteenth century, new life came to a remote little port called Cardiff. Cardiff was a fishing and market town of just over 1,000 folk, centred on a Norman keep where the River Taff enters the Severn. It might well have stayed small like Looe or Brixham, but Merthyr Tydfil and other settlements behind it had already begun to produce coal and iron. Cardiff became their port, growing into a major city and, in Edwardian times, the world's largest exporter of coal. When coal declined new industries developed down on the docks – for example this huge steel complex that has given employment for decades. The old East Moors steelworks (centre) was demolished shortly after this picture was taken in 1977. Now Allied Steel and Wire Ltd makes steel in its modern works at Tremorfa (just beyond, right), and processes it in the new Castle Works alongside Bute East Dock (foreground).

Whitford Point, West Glamorgan

South Wales concentrates its industrial efforts in the valleys and at half a dozen busy, breath-taking centres along the coast. But drift just a few kilometres away from this complex in almost any direction, and you'll soon find yourself in an older, cleaner and altogether gentler Wales. Whitford Burrows, for example, is a National Trust reserve, one of many coastal reserves on the exquisite Gower Peninsula. Remote and unspoiled, it is only six kilometres (less than four miles) from Llanelli's tinplate works, and less than 20 kilometres (12 miles) from the centre of Swansea. Bought through Enterprise Neptune Fund, an appeal of the National Trust for coastal conservation, it stands on the north Gower shore in the Loughor Estuary. Whitford Burrows is a wild, sandy peninsula of sea grasses and saltings. Whitford Sands, on one side, and Llanrhidian Sands on the other are tidal flats, covered twice every day by the sea and rich in crabs, molluscs, worms, and the sea birds and shore birds that feed on them. The lighthouse stands on sandbanks just off the end of the Burrows. Once it shone brightly to keep ships on course, but nobody seems interested any more.

Tenby, Dyfed

At first glance Tenby seems rather like St Ives, but take another look. Those are villas, rather than fishermen's cottages, and they tell of a much more prosperous merchant community than ever lived near Land's End. With its sheltered, cosy harbour Tenby was a flourishing port in Tudor times and even before; its protective walls and castle were probably started in the twelfth century. The reason for its decline is all too clear in this picture – the harbour dries out at low tide and is unsuitable for anything bigger than small coasting vessels or fishing smacks. However, Tenby prospered as a port for local produce, coastal trading and fishing well into the nineteenth century. The railway that finally killed off the coasters brought holiday-makers instead, so Tenby has continued on its sleepy, happy way, now as a coastal resort. St Catherine's Island (background) has a small mid-Victorian fort – part of the south-coast defences against the French.

Pembroke, Dyfed

Built along a chalk ridge on the banks of a tidal stream, Pembroke is dominated by its splendid Norman castle, where the Earls of Pembroke once lived. Castle and town walls were built about 1093. The round keep, 23 metres (75 feet) high, dating from about 1200, was strong enough to withstand Cromwell for seven weeks when he besieged it over four centuries later. Only fragments of the town wall still remain (there are some at the bottom of the picture). A sleepy little town, Pembroke is a market centre for this southern corner of its county, and a popular holiday centre with a reputation for warmth and sunshine. Though Pembroke River opens into the south side of Milford Haven, the town long ago gave up any pretence of being a port. Industrial development was not ignored; it was simply diverted to neighbouring Pembroke Dock, some three kilometres (two miles) away to the north-west. Opened as a naval dockyard in the early nineteenth century, and now an industrial suburb, Pembroke Dock has successfully absorbed all the ugliness that might have invaded – and ruined – Pembroke itself.

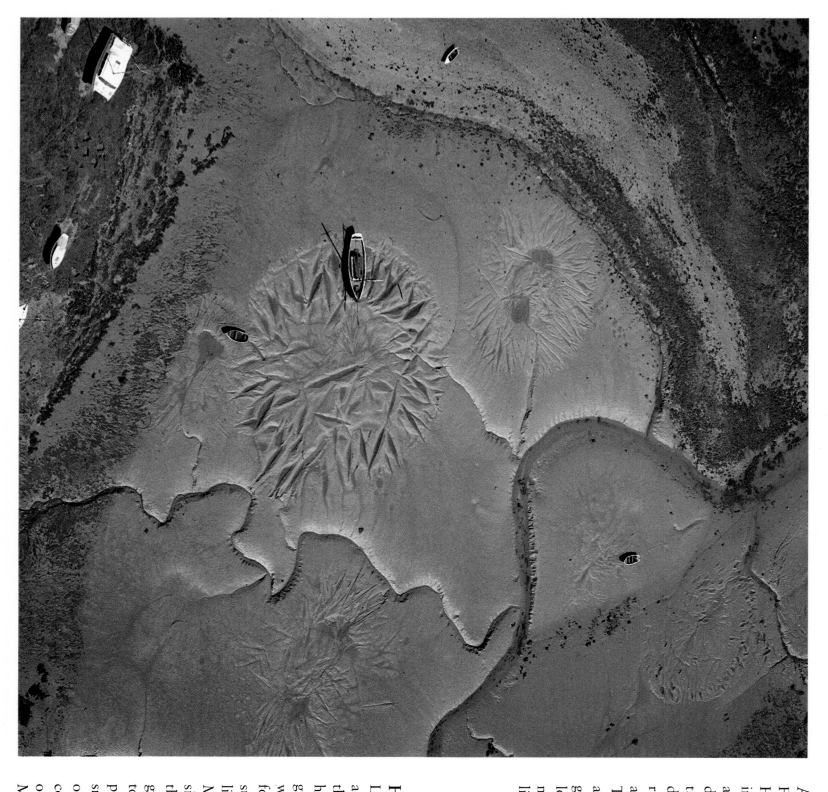

Angle, Dyfed

From its quiet corner at the southern entrance to Milford Haven, Angle holds its breath and watches as the oil industry grows. The tankers in the channel have doubled and redoubled in size; the freighters passing up and down have multiplied. There's a huddle of huge storage tanks just across the bay at Rhoscrowther; there are two deep-water jetties just around the point and another reaches out from the far side of the Haven. At night they all light up like Christmas trees. So far everything is fine. There's a film of oil on the water that wasn't there before, and a scare every now and again when some ass lets a few gallons loose in the harbour. But even a little oil goes a long way, and a lot of oil could make a mess — an awful mess — down here on the shore where the people of Angle like to moor their boats.

Haverfordwest, Dyfed

Like many county towns of Britain, Haverfordwest long ago earned the right to an annual fair. In fact it has two — the May Fair in spring and Portfield Fair in autumn. It has managed, through centuries of change, to keep a green broad enough to hold its fairs, even modern ones with roundabouts, swings and sideshows. A natural focal point for the Pembroke peninsula, Haverfordwest stands on a mound above the Western Cleddau River, linked to the sea through the sheltered tidal waters of Milford Haven. Roads converge on the town from all sides. Defended by a castle, it grew in importance through medieval times. It was for long the main western gateway to Ireland, and Henry VIII declared it both a town and county in its own right. As ships grew bigger its prosperity declined, for the Western Cleddau is only a small river. Now Fishguard and Milford Haven have overtaken it, but Haverfordwest still has its memories, its comfortable role in county matters and its colourful fair on St Thomas's Green. And despite its lack of ships, its Mayor is still Port Admiral.

Aberystwyth, Dyfed

Built where two rivers flow into Cardigan Bay, overlooked by an Iron Age hilltop fort (bottom right), Aberystwyth is a holiday town with a difference. The Normans built a castle on the crags above the north beach, where the ground plan can still be seen (top left). The town spread out below, gradually becoming a port as the need arose. Diverting the River Ystwyth (bottom) into the mouth of the larger River Rheidol helped to keep the harbour entrance clear, and the moles gave protection in all weathers. Aberystwyth traded with Ireland and points on the British coast. It carried lead from the mines inland, and even exported Welshmen directly to the Americas. By the late nineteenth century it was established as an administrative centre for its area and a staid University town. As the port declined the holiday traffic grew, but Aberystwyth kept its sense of responsibility. While Colwyn Bay and Llandudno became the Skegness and Blackpool of North Wales, Aberystwyth took on a quieter, more appropriate role — the Eastbourne of Cardigan Bay.

Aberdovey, Gwynedd

The mountains that sweep down to central Cardigan Bay are cut by two major estuaries; Aberystwyth is built on one, Aberdovey on the other. This little town drapes itself along the narrow shore on the north-western corner of the Dovey or Dyfi estuary, climbing the hill to catch as much sun – and see as far across the water – as possible. At high tide the estuary is a triangular expanse of shallow sea, at low tide a huge acreage of golden-yellow sand. Waders and wildfowl gather there from miles around to feed as the water surges in or out past the protective sand-spit of Ynyslas. Aberdovey has no aspirations and few pretensions. It is not a port, though it has a landing stage and can give shelter to fishing boats when the wind is right. It is a great centre for sailing and quiet holidays, and for speculating about the past. At low spring tides, when the wind blows off the land, you can see patches of ancient tree stumps extending out to sea – remnants of a forest that stretched out into Cardigan Bay 7,000 to 10,000 years ago. With imagination you may even hear bells – the legendary bells of Aberdovey – calling you to church far out in the drowned forest.

Snowdonia, Gwynedd

Snowdon and its companions form a magnificent huddle in the north-western corner of Wales. Snowdon rises to 1,085 metres (3,560 feet); from it run five sharp ridges with lesser peaks spread out along them. Here we are cruising above the summit (you can just make it out on the right) and looking south-eastward along Bwlchy-soethau to Y Lliwedd, just less than 900 metres (2,925 feet) high. The lakes in the corrie are Glaslyn and Llyn Llydaw. Gallt y Wenallt stands beyond the further lake, and the valley behind is Nantgwynant, with the Watkin path – one of the easier routes for hikers – snaking up the hillside toward the ridge. On a sunny summer day like this it looks bland, almost benevolent, but in winter Snowdonia is a deathtrap. Every year it claims victims from climbers and hikers, who, tempted by its majesty, go just a little too far. The miners and quarrymen who worked Snowdonia in Victorian times, winter and summer alike, must have been hardy folk indeed.

Caernarfon, Gwynedd

Caernarvon town stands on the Welsh mainland, at a point where two rivers join to enter the Menai Strait. It commands the south-western end of the Strait, which is considerably restricted by sandbanks along the Anglesey shore. The Romans, who had an eye for such things, built their fort Segontium on a hillside above the town. The present castle stands on the site of an older motte-and-bailey. Caernarvon Castle is every small boy's idea of what a castle should look like, with curtain walls, battlements and towers at every corner. There was even a drawbridge. Edward I planned it in 1283 as a military headquarters for the control of Wales. His designer may have been inspired by castles seen on the Crusades, for the shapes of some of the towers and the decorative colour-banding have an eastern flavour – reminiscent of Constantinople, some say. Work on the castle stopped abruptly when Welsh dissidents (who were probably paying through the nose for it) moved in and began to take it apart. Eventually completed, as much as any castle is ever completed, it cost £27,000, and was worth every penny at that.

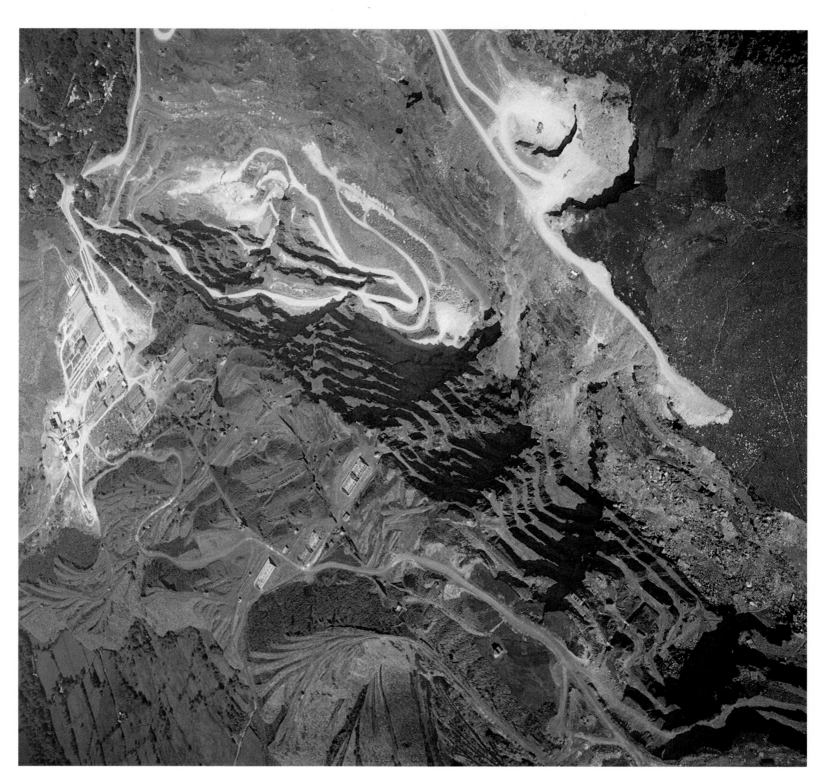

Menai Bridge, Gwynedd

Thomas Telford was never up in a balloon; it is all the more remarkable that his Menai Strait Bridge should look as utterly right from the air as it does from the ground. He built it between 1818 and 1826 to carry his London-to-Holyhead highway over the Strait. The road had to be high, for Menai was a busy waterway and tall ships with masts of 30 metres (100 feet) and more needed to pass. The leap over to Anglesey was a long one for bridge-builders of the time. So Telford's team designed and built the first of the modern suspension bridges. Taking off cleverly from the cliffs on the mainland side (right) kept the bridge high. Making use of a well-placed reef on the Anglesey shore kept the main span down to 177 metres (580 feet). The granite towers stood four-square on rock at either end, and the weight of the deck – a double carriage-way – was taken by huge wrought-iron chains. These lasted well over a century before being replaced with modern steel cables.

Bethesda, Gwynedd

The quarries took their name from the village, which grew up in early Victorian times about a Bethesda Congregational Chapel. Chapel and slates between them dominated the lives of the hardy folk who were proud to be called quarrymen. Welsh slates come in all sizes and colours, and Bethesda's were ever among the finest. Grey, green, red and blue, they were dug out, split and shaped in the long quarry houses, and exported from Bethesda by the million. Many went out to the ends of the earth from Port Penrhyn, on the Menai Strait, that was owned (like the quarries themselves) by Lord Penrhyn of Penrhyn Castle. The Castle, now National Trust property, is tastefully decorated with artefacts of slate, including an oversized slate bedstead. As the quarries grew deeper the spoil-tips spread, for slate-trimming is an extravagant business that takes the best and leaves the dross. Extravagant too in human lives, it confers silicosis (quarryman's lung) on those who chip slates too long, giving them an early, wheezing death. Just round the corner and up the road however, is the Nant Ffrancon Pass, pointing the way to Snowdonia and some of the finest scenery in Wales.

Conwy, Gwynedd

Tucked away in its corner south of Great Ormes Head, Conwy (or Conway) can easily be overlooked. Only a small town, with population of twelve thousand or so, it is overshadowed by neighbouring Llandudno and Colwyn Bay, and less authoritative than Caernarfon or Bangor. So what has Conwy to distinguish it? Surprisingly, it carries enormous weight with historians. The castle, which looks far too good to be true, is the genuine thirteenth-century article and of unusual design appropriate to its difficult site. Conwy itself is an almost perfect example of a planned medieval town (rare in Europe as a whole) and with most of its walls still intact after six centuries of wear and tear. The castle was well designed with economy of manpower in mind: it could be defended completely by a very small force. More important, the little town alongside soon grew fat enough to burst out of its walls, and has been growing slowly and gracefully ever since. Telford built the matching suspension bridge for the coach road, and Robert Stephenson designed the tubular railway bridge, and whoever built the new bridge did a good job too.

Gronant, near Prestatyn, Clwyd

The sand that chokes the River Dee spills round the corner to this northern coast of Wales. At low tide in summer, when the sandbanks dry out in the sun and the wind blows on-shore, you can see the surface rippling and lifting, and the sand shifting bodily toward the land. So dunes are formed, like the line of mature, grass-covered mounds in the background. The coastal fields themselves are probably sand (to judge by the way they have dried out) and fit only to park caravans on. Prestatyn came late into the holiday business. It was a small industrial town, with lead its main preoccupation almost to the end of the nineteenth century. Now it is one big holiday resort, with good beaches and plenty of man-made amusements in the centre. Like the rest of the north Welsh resorts, it caters mainly for the crowds from industrial Lancashire and West Yorkshire, competing with Benidorm and the Costa del Sol for their continuing attention.

Castell Dinas Bran, Clwyd

Almost one and a half kilometres (about a mile) from Llangollen on the edge of North Wales, Castell Dinas Bran dominates the valley of the Dee. Built about the eighth century on a mound that must certainly have seen earlier battles, it was a bastion of the Celtic twilight – a stronghold for Welsh settlers against Saxon slave-raiders and rustlers from the east. Later the Welsh fought the Norman French, over the same ground, and later still the English, but by then Dinas Bran was outmoded – as irrelevant for battle as Caernarvon Castle is today. Madoc ap Gruffydd, who owned it in the thirteenth century, founded the abbey of Valle Crucis nearby. The limestone escarpment, Creigiau Eglwyseg, marks another, much older invasion from the east – that of a warm sea which lapped in Carboniferous times against the ancient Silurian heartland of Wales. Among its legacies are the coal measures and limestone rocks that have brought prosperity to both southern and northern ends of the Principality. In July the crags, even Dinas Bran itself, ring with music, for Llangollen is the home of the annual International Eisteddfod.

Chirk Castle, Denbigh

Chirk is a different kind of castle, built by Roger Mortimer in the time of Edward I and, like many castles, never completed. Edward himself took responsibility for building the more important castles in his defence line. Lesser ones along the English-Welsh border he began, then handed them over half-finished to landowners who he expected would complete them. Begun in 1282, Chirk was only half-built when Mortimer fell from grace. Money and initiative ran out, so the castle stuck at only half its projected size, with stumpy incomplete towers. In the Civil War it was held as a Royalist stronghold by Sir John Watts, against its owner Sir Thomas Myddleton. Later General Lambert and his Parliamentary force blasted one side away. Fortunately nobody thought to reduce it further; it survived as a private dwelling and has been lived in almost continuously by the Myddelton family ever since.

Shrewsbury, Shropshire

The Severn begins on the slopes of Plynlimon, not far from Aberdovey. By the time it has reached Montgomery, less than a quarter of its journey done, it already seems an old, tired river, winding wearily along a well-worn path. Through Shropshire it staggers to and fro, in everlasting argument with itself over which way to go. North of the Long Mynd it makes up its mind, crossing the plain south-eastward in huge, graceful loops like a rope flaked over a deck. In one of the loops – a particularly tight one – stands Shrewsbury. Almost ringed by river, the site of Shrewsbury has been fortified since the fifth century, if not before. It became a village when the people of nearby Viroconium moved there after the Roman legions withdrew. Welsh and British fought round it in pre-Norman times. Already a town by the time of the Domesday survey, it acquired a castle in the twelfth century and later a wall (parts of which you see bounding the old town in this photograph). Shrewsbury is a meeting point of many major routes. Anyone coming near it wants to drop in and see its medieval streets and houses and that leads to traffic problems in the near-island inner city. The railway wisely stayed outside.

Iron Bridge, Shropshire

South-east from Shrewsbury the Severn takes on a new determination, following a narrow gorge through the limestone ridges of eastern Shropshire. Coal and ironstone drew early settlers to the area, and small-scale mining and smelting were carried on side by side for centuries. In 1709 Abraham Darby, a local ironmaster, invented coke-smelting, and – until the coal ran out – these wooded hills reeked with the fumes and grime of a huge iron-founding industry. Between 1779 and 1781 Darby's foundry cast the Iron Bridge, designed by Thomas Pritchard to show what could be done with iron as a building material. The delicate webbing of the main arch spans over 30 metres (100 feet). It was a magnificent advertisement and a whole new concept of iron founding and construction developed from it. Here we drift eastward over Coalbrookdale and the township that grew up alongside the Iron Bridge.

Leek, Staffordshire

Just a field under the snow, but brown elms, blue shadows and low afternoon sun make magic for the photographer. It is only a light fall late in March, and it has hardly drifted at all, so there's not much danger for the stock. But there's not much feed either, and it's close to lambing time. More work for the farmer.

Little Moreton Hall, Cheshire

This remarkable house stands alone on its moated island between Congleton and Kidgrove, on the lush plain of eastern Cheshire. The site was probably owned by the Moreton family as early as the thirteenth century, and the present house, started about 1480, almost certainly replaced an earlier one. It is a perfect example of a timber-framed farm house, of the kind found in many corners of Britain where stone and brick were scarce, but timber – oak for preference – was plentiful. The earliest part is the H-shaped block at the back – a large, barn-like hall with two-storied wings at either end. In the mid-sixteenth century William Moreton modernized it, splitting the hall with an upper floor, and building on bay windows with huge, leaded lights. Later the south-facing front was added, with its gatehouse, chapel and long oak-lined gallery where the family could promenade in winter. The extra fire-places with their brick-work chimneys date from this period. Little Moreton Hall was never a palace. It was a family house for fairly prosperous landowners, who in later generations divided their lives between Cheshire and London. At times it suffered neglect, but it was lived in, mostly by Moretons, up to the early years of the present century. The timbers have shifted slightly; nothing is square to anything else, and the National Trust (who took it over in 1937) have had some shoring-up and strengthening to do. For a timber-and-wattle building up to 500 years old, Little Moreton Hall is looking fine, and shaping up well for whatever the next few centuries may bring.

Chester, Cheshire

Like Shrewsbury, Chester was built in the bend of a river, on a slight rise that lifts it above the flood plain. As its name suggests, the Romans chose this site at the head of the Dee Estuary for a fort, and the Mercians and Normans who followed could only agree with their choice. In 1254 the 15-year-old Prince Edward was made Earl of Chester by his father Henry III; later as Edward I he developed the town and used it as a headquarters for his campaigns in Wales. Up to the eighteenth century it was a port, and quite an important one, for trading across the Irish Sea. Then its river let Chester down: too sluggish for its own good, it allowed the channels in the sandy estuary to silt up. The upstart port of Liverpool took over. Chester's inner city still has its entire walls, some sections dating back to Roman times. The original Roman street plan lives on in the centre and a large Roman amphitheatre has been excavated just outside the wall near Newgate. The sandstone cathedral is relatively modern, dating from the fourteenth century. Its roof forms a jade cross (to right of centre in this picture). It looks like a day at the races for the people of Chester, in their splendidly sited racecourse south-west of the city.

Birkenhead, Merseyside

For most of the time that Chester was a flourishing port, Birkenhead was a tiny hamlet of no more than 100 souls – a ferry point close to a Benedictine priory in a forested corner of the Wirral peninsula. So it remained until the early nineteenth century, when the citizens of overcrowded Liverpool began to look enviously at the unspoiled shore across the Mersey. A steam ferry service was inaugurated, and in 1824 a boiler-maker called William Laird moved over to Wallasey Creek, a sheltered arm of the estuary on the Wirral side. There he set up workshops and a shipyard for building his new, experimental, riveted iron ships. With help from a Scottish designer, Laird laid out a new town on a grid plan reminiscent of the new Edinburgh. Hamilton Square, seen here in the centre, retains some of the character of his concept, but bombing, development and other devastations have left little of it intact. The town hall was interposed on the south-east side of the square in the 1880s. Birkenhead has grown and thrived, mainly on shipbuilding and allied industries, spreading gradually to fill the whole north-eastern corner of the Wirral from Bebbington to New Brighton.

Liverpool, Merseyside

By no means the loveliest of cities, Liverpool grew with a rush during the late eighteenth and nineteenth centuries. Industrial expediency and money-grubbing could have made it a complete disaster, but something – fierce civic pride perhaps – said no. Hard times have come upon it, but Liverpool is still a big city – one that generates a strong feeling of belonging among its heterogeneous population. It grew slowly through the Middle Ages, from a small fishing village on a tidal pool to a busy, easily accessible port for sailing ships plying to the Americas. By the early eighteenth century it had three kilometres (about two miles) of dock basins and a busy trade with New England and the Caribbean. Then ships grew bigger, and while others failed, Liverpool came into its own. During the late nineteenth and early twentieth centuries it became Britain's second largest deep-water port for ocean liners. Its dock area doubled and redoubled, and most of its important buildings date from that period. Many of the famous ones can be seen here, including the waterfront trio of Royal Liver Building (with two towers), Mersey Docks and Harbour Board Building (copper dome), and the lower Cunard Building between. The long striped slugs are Lime Street Station, better known by its railway-Gothic facade. The many-columned creation beyond is St George's Hall, and some of Liverpool's new housing developments can be seen on the right. The coronet in the right foreground is the new Roman Catholic Cathedral, one of the few cathedrals of any denomination with a car park under its nave.

Runcorn, Cheshire

The guidebooks have little or nothing to say about Runcorn, an honest little port and centre for chemical industry at the head of the Mersey estuary. Its high-arched railway bridge over the river and the Manchester Ship Canal is a landmark just off the main road from Manchester to North Wales. You cross the lower road bridge alongside if you are diverting to Widnes or Liverpool. Not normally to be thought of as Britain's most beautiful corner, there is magic even in Runcorn when the fog hangs low, the factory smoke rises, and shadows are long in the November sun.

Fiddler's Ferry, Cheshire

If early winter sunshine and fog can make a fairyland of Runcorn, it can do the same for Warrington just a few kilometres north-west along the river. Here Fiddler's Ferry, the enormous power station outside Warrington, is transformed by the same bright magic.

Manchester, Greater Manchester

Begun by the Romans on the plains of the Irwell River, Manchester had no natural seaport facilities. It was sheer northern brass neck that developed the Ship Canal, making the city an inland port that could compete on its own terms with Liverpool, London and the rest. Though cotton-spinning and weaving were the mainstays of its nineteenth-century development, Manchester's lively population (many of them immigrants from Europe) developed a diversity of skills that have helped to keep the city going, now that cotton is no longer king. Here is a small section of the city centre, with (inset) the excellent circular Central Library, built in the 1930s, and the triangular block of the Victorian Gothic Town Hall. Old and new buildings seem to blend particularly well in Manchester (inset), especially since both were cleansed of their grime.

Leyland Vehicle Test Track, Lancashire

British Leyland, perhaps the biggest name in British automobile manufacture, takes its name from a small town a few kilometres south of Preston. Since its inception, the firm of Leyland Motors specialized in heavy goods vehicles and motor buses, diversifying into tanks and armoured carriers during the Second World War. Though linked in various ways with other, more volatile branches of the automotive industry, the name Leyland continues to be associated with the heavy end of the market. At Leyland itself they have soldiered on through industrial crisis, concentrating on what they do best. Here is the test track, close to Leyland town, where the buses and goods vehicles are checked for stability and roadworthiness on a circuit of bumps, skid-pans and graded corners.

Blackpool, Lancashire

As the mill-towns of Lancashire began to prosper from the late eighteenth century onward, first the owners and then the workforce dreamed of holidays away from the grime and clutter of the looms. Lancashire's sea coast, well endowed with fresh air and golden sandy beaches, was the obvious outlet. If the wealthy minority wanted peace and quiet during their brief holidays, they could be accommodated with ease; Lytham St Annes and Southport were built for them. If the poorer majority preferred noise, bustle and entertainment, in compensation for the drabness of their lives in the mill, that could be arranged too; Blackpool, and later Morecambe and Heysham, were the answers. Blackpool, a tiny fishing village in the early nineteenth century, became renowned first for its bathing and bracing air through the writings of the scientist William Hutton, to whom sea water was an elixir and cure-all. It grew rapidly after the railway arrived, with boarding houses, hotels, theatres and entertainments laid on mainly for summer crowds. The Tower, built in 1895, is a slightly-more-than-half-sized version of the Eiffel Tower. Almost 160 metres (518 feet) high, it affords splendid views in all directions and has a zoo, circus, ballroom and theatre organ in the base. Blackpool is believed to entertain some 8,000,000 visitors every year.

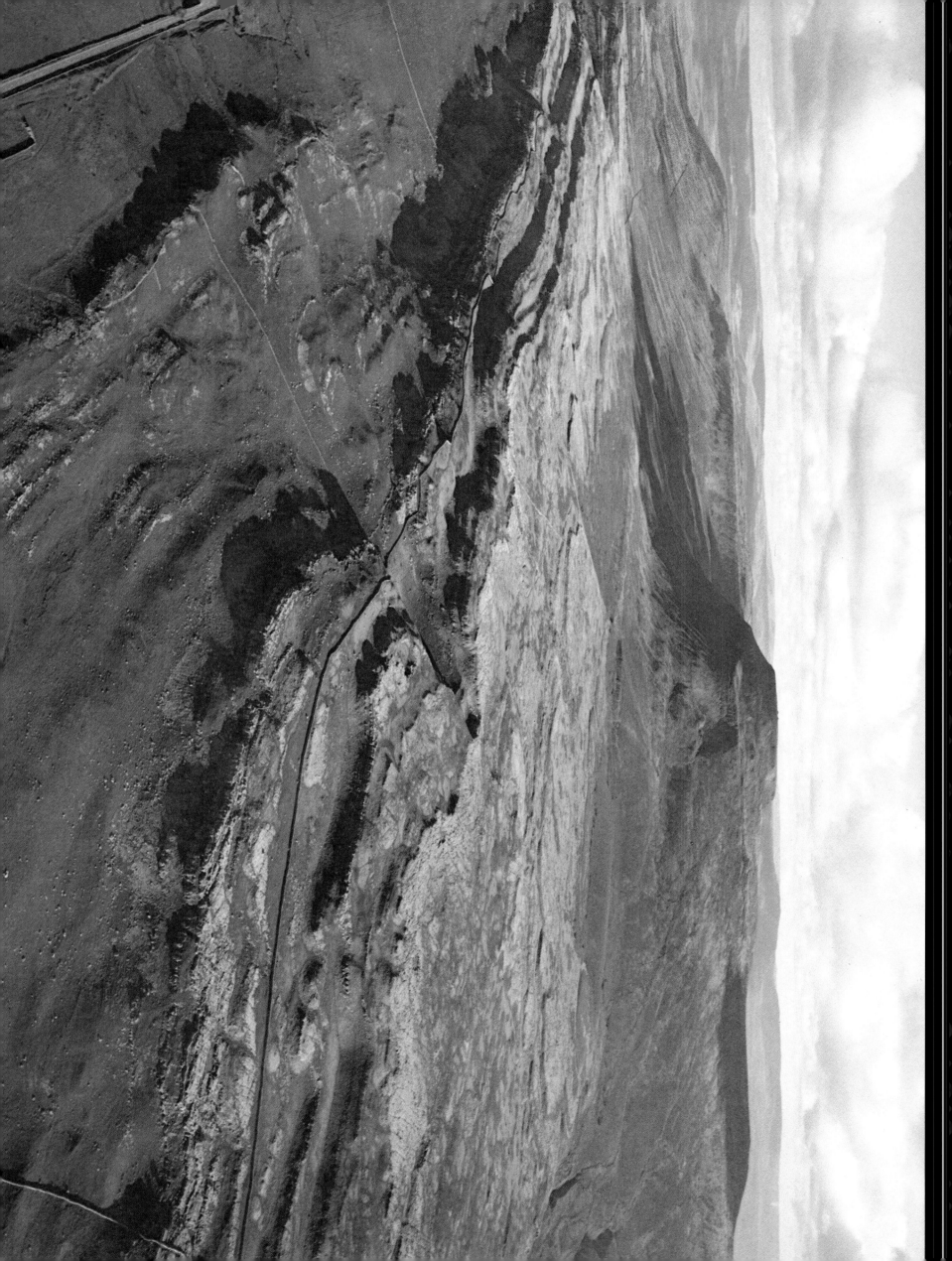

Raven Scar, North Yorkshire

The scar limestones, part of the Carboniferous or coal-bearing series of rocks, were laid down over 300 million years ago as sediments on the bed of a warm, shallow sea. Now they stand 300 metres (1,000 feet) and more above sea level, their near-horizontal strata eroded into steps by frost and rain. Here in North Yorkshire limestone terraces like Raven Scar provide much of the scenery between Settle and Malham. Erosion affects them internally too, for this is a region where streams disappear like rabbits into the ground and hollow out huge cathedral-sized caverns below the surface. Potholers disappear after them, for beneath the hillsides are systems of tunnels and shafts that enthusiasts cross the world to visit. In the background is Ingleborough, a cap of tougher shales and millstone grit that rises to 723 metres (2,373 feet). There is an Iron Age fort on top, and usually a crowd of climbers, hikers, scouts, Royal Marine commandos and others who have shinned up in their various ways to admire the view. Dedicated fell-runners take in Ingleborough and its two neighbouring peaks – Whernside and Pen-y-ghent – in a single trot.

Ingleton, North Yorkshire

Just round the corner and a few hundred metres below Raven Scar, the village of Ingleton nestles in a valley where two streams meet. Formerly a mining centre, Ingleton was the home of lead-miners, coal-miners and quarrymen who delved into the hills above. The railway from Clapham made it accessible to a wider public, who discovered North Yorkshire and used Ingleton as a centre for exploration. Now more than anything else it is a focal point for climbers, potholers and fell-walkers, for whom this corner of the Yorkshire Dales National Park provides year-round attraction. Whernside (737 metres, 2,419 feet) rises behind the village, surrounded by its skirt of scar limestones, and the lower slopes of Ingleborough appear on the right. The arched viaduct that took the railway on to Sedbergh and Penrith is no longer in use, but the road in the foreground, the A65 from Settle to Kendal, is one of the busiest in the north throughout the summer.

Bowness, Cumbria

It is hard to tell where Windermere town ends and Bowness begins. However it doesn't really matter—they are both pleasant little settlements on the eastern shore of Windermere, comfortable rather than distinguished, and crowded with tourists in summer. There wasn't much of either before the mid-nineteenth century. Until that time the Lakes were hard to reach, and the lakeland poets were among the few who appreciated them. Then, in 1847, the railway arrived. Both towns became centres for holiday-makers, not the proletariat from the cotton towns, but rather the slightly up-market kind, who liked fell-walking and sailing, bird-watching and Words-worth, and comfortable digs with prime Cumberland sausages at the end of the day. Bowness is a port for the thousand-and-more sailing craft that tack to and fro on Windermere, and for the ferries that ply up, down and across the lake. Here we look south along the lake toward Newby Bridge and Morecambe Bay. Just over on the west side is Beatrix Potter country. Jemima Puddleduck, Mrs Tiggy-Winkle and a host of other characters from her books were immortalized in this area. Later, their creator came to settle at Hill Top, near Sawrey, a few kilometres to the south-west.

Boretree Tarn, Cumbria

The delight of the Lake District owes just as much to its little lakes as its big ones. When the glaciers were active 20,000 years ago they scoured both wide and deep, leaving a roller-coaster relief in the hard bed-rock. High rainfall (and Cumbria has about the highest rainfall in England) does the rest. Wherever there is a hollow, it fills with water to form a tarn. The valleys among the main lakes are dotted with tiny tarns that shine like jewels and add much to any Lake District panorama. Here we look down over Boretree Tarn, on Yew Barrow in Furness Fells, close to Newby Bridge at the southern end of Windermere. On the left the ground rises to Grizedale forest, with Coniston fells beyond.

Brackenthwaite Fell, Cumbria

It rises steeply out of the dark, enclosed, glacial valley of Crummock Water to 851 metres (2,791 feet) above sea level. The highest peak in this north-western section of the Lake District, Brackenthwaite's steep paths are a delight for fell-walkers and its crags a challenge to climbers. From the top on a clear day you can look east-north-eastward – more or less the way we are looking now – and see right across to Helvellyn. Here we can look down into Keswick and Derwent Water as well. At the foot of the Fell is the B5289, heading from Cockermouth and the industrial north-west toward Keswick. It passes along the shore of Crummock Water, rounding Hause Point to the village of Buttermere (on the delta, between lakes), then rises well above Buttermere and leaves the valley eastward by Honister Pass.

Ennerdale Water, Cumbria

Windermere, Thirlmere, Derwent Water and many other lakes are ringed by roads and haunted by holidaymakers. Not so Ennerdale Water; it is one of the remotest and most difficult to reach, well over to the west. From Ennerdale Bridge you may have to walk nearly two kilometres (about a mile) to reach its rather sombre shores, and that is more than most casual visitors are prepared to do. However, from the roadhead, about six kilometres (nearly four miles) further on, it is only a short walk. Like so many other lakes, it lies in a steep-sided valley, cut by one of the glaciers that radiated from Cumbria's former ice dome. Its flanks, mostly wooded at the eastern end, fall steeply into the lake. For those who know them there are tracks, rewarding scrambles on the high fells, and climbs among the hard-rock crags in the dale beyond. Looking up the lake from the western end, Ennerdale Fell rises to the right, Ennerdale Forest to the left. The high mound of Pillar (892 metres, 2,927 feet) stands clear on the skyline.

Dumfries, Dumfries and Galloway Region

This is a prosperous corner of Scotland – low-lying, well-watered, with fertile soils and a gentle climate. Dumfries is its ancient capital, a former county town and a royal burgh since 1186. The town arose on a Bronze Age site on the banks of the River Nith. Its history is turbulent. There were English raids and private wars between rival landowners lasting well into the sixteenth century. Peace came with the Act of Union, disturbed only by Prince Charlie, who held Dumfries briefly in 1745. Marketing, spinning, weaving and knitting became the mainstays of the town's prosperity, and it has diversified into milk processing and chemicals. Here below us is the River Nith, winding southward with the town on either side. The hill on the right is Criffel, and the coastal hills of Cumbria rise in the far distance across Solway Firth.

Motherwell, Strathclyde Region

Motherwell and Wishaw together make up a large industrial town on the Clyde south-east of Glasgow. The combination of coal, iron-stone and water dictated their development during the eighteenth century, after an ironmaster came up from Sheffield to establish the first Scottish ironworks at Carron. The industry spread to the Lanarkshire coal-field, for the local splint coals suited the furnaces and there were rich ores close by. When the iron ore ran out, the iron and steel industry continued to develop using imported ores, with new processes replacing old, and fierce competition eliminating all but the most efficient. The huge Ravenscraig complex east of Motherwell, developed between the wars, manufactures and rolls steel, sending it out as coiled strip. Here is Ravenscraig in full blast – one of British Steel Corporation's success stories, employing a work force of 5,000.

Glasgow, Strathclyde Region

A port on the Clyde for many centuries, Glasgow grew enormously during the Victorian era. The poverty of the Highlands was its making, for immigrants from the glens, landless and starving, flocked to find work in the city and fill its appalling tenements south of the river. The Irish connection too has long been there, for Glasgow and Northern Ireland are close in many ways. Scotland's largest city by far, Glasgow and its suburbs together hold about half the country's population, but it has never aspired to be a capital except in the commercial sense. Its civic pride is strong – Glasgow has many fine parks and public buildings and has done more than many other British cities to rid itself of its slums. Here we approach the city from the south-east along the Clyde: that's Glasgow Green – one of the larger parks – in the foreground with London Road flanking it. Down on the left is the Gorbals area, all that remains of a notorious Victorian slum. On the north bank of the river are Custom House Quay, Broomielaw and Anderston Quay, with Kingston Bridge carrying the M8 over the river. In the middle distance lie Kelvingrove Park and the attractive north-western suburbs. Beyond are Bearsden, Milngavie and the ancient volcanic stumps of the Kilpatrick Hills.

Loch Lomond, Strathclyde Region

Almost two-and-a-half times the length of Windermere, Loch Lomond is Britain's largest lake, some 37 kilometres (23 miles) long and up to eight kilometres (5 miles) wide at its southern end. Loch Lomond stands only about six metres (20 feet) above sea level, but the glaciers that gouged it did a thorough job; at its deepest, toward the northern end, it plunges to almost 200 metres (630 feet). There are several inlets, and the River Leven drains it into the Firth of Clyde at Dumbarton. Considering its proximity to Clydeside, Loch Lomond remains remarkably unspoilt. Perhaps the Clyde ferries that took day-trippers to Rothesay and Dunoon diverted local attention from it. That is the main road, the A82, along much of its western shore, and visitors drive from all parts of Britain just to see this most famous of all Scottish lochs. Usually there is a procession of them driving slowly just ahead of you along the narrow, winding road, especially if you are in a hurry to get from Glasgow to the Western Highlands. Here we drift over the southern end of Loch Lomond, looking northward to Inchmurrin and the lesser islands beyond. Ben Lomond (974 metres, 3,194 feet) rises to the east, just beyond the narrows of Rubha Mór.

84

The Crinan Canal, Strathclyde Region

Linking the Sound of Jura with Loch Fyne, the Crinan Canal was designed to shorten the sea route from the Clyde to the Western Isles. By avoiding the long and often dangerous run around the Mull of Kintyre, sailing ships could reduce the journey from Glasgow by days or even weeks. Construction began in 1794, and the canal opened for business seven years later. In 1816 Thomas Telford, Britain's greatest civil engineer, was brought in to refurbish it, and the canal was reopened in more or less its present form in 1817. It runs north-eastward from Ardrishaig on Loch Gilp (a side-arm of Loch Fyne) to Crinan on the Sound of Jura, a distance of about 14 kilometres (nine miles). Never less than 12 metres (40 feet) across and three metres (ten feet) deep, it rises to 20 metres (66 feet) above sea level, with 15 locks scattered along its length. Here we look down on the high locks at Barnakill, and the long, straight stretch to Cairnbaan. The Crinan Canal has carried many fishing boats and small coasters in its time, but yachtsmen use it more than anyone else these days.

Inveraray, Strathclyde Region

Near the point where the River Aray runs into Loch Fyne stands this tiny Georgian township, the Royal Burgh of Inveraray. It was built during the second half of the eighteenth century by the third Duke of Argyll, on the site of a much older settlement that was burnt by Royalist forces in the 1644 rising. Inveraray and its nearby castle, built about the same time, form the hereditary seat of the Campbells of Argyll. The quay is a reminder that Loch Fyne, a narrow sea-loch, provided the main route to Inveraray well into the present century. The roads were mere tracks that travellers avoided if they could. Visitors and stores arrived by sailing ships and latterly by 'puffers' – small, coal-fired steamers that are still remembered with great affection throughout the west of Scotland.

Ben Nevis, Highland Region

Not the most beautiful, and far from the most spectacular of Britain's mountains, Ben Nevis has but one claim to fame; at 1,344 metres (4,406 feet) it is the highest. Crowded to east and south by lesser peaks, it stands like a lumpen sentinel at the gate of the Great Glen, glowering over Loch Linnhe and keeping the morning sun off Fort William. Its lower flanks are of granite and gneiss; the upper half is a capping of porphyritic greenstone, poured over from a neighbouring volcano when the world was younger. It is the greenstone that breaks to form spectacular cliffs and crags on the north-eastern face. The summit is a plateau – a fairly crowded plateau on fine summer days when the tourists rise. Some climb the easy way, up the bridle path that winds its way up the western face (to the right of the picture). Others take a harder route up the crags. All who get to the top stare sadly at the ruins of the observatory and small hotel, and wish that one or other were still open to serve refreshments.

Great Glen, Highland Region

Over 160 kilometres (100 miles) long from Mull to Moray Firth, Glen Mor nan Albyn – the Great Glen – cuts a swathe through Scotland's oldest and highest mountains. The Glen is a fault-line – a plane of movement between two sliding blocks that move further out of alignment with each passing year. Lined with ancient tracks, it has long formed a highway for animals and people; when General Wade built the road for his Redcoats he was following well-worn routes. You can see the road winding across Laggan delta and crossing the bridge before Loch Oich. In happier times a century later Thomas Telford built the Caledonian Canal. Cutting through 35 kilometres (22 miles) of rocks created a 96 kilometre (60 mile) waterway. Opened in 1822, the canal was designed to link Inverness and the north with Fort William and the south. This is the centre section, just over 30 metres (one hundred feet) above sea level. It was never a commercial success, but fishermen and holiday makers use it happily.

Mallaig, Highland Region

If the far Cuillin of Skye are putting love on you, as the song says, the traditional road to get you there is the Road to the Isles. There's a good motor road these days by Loch Tummel and Loch Rannoch, but there it turns into a track, and you won't get much further without a cromag. Indeed if you are driving you'll do better to go on the longer route through Dalwhinnie and Fort William. Either way you end up on the isolated Morar peninsula, and eventually at the little town of Mallaig. One of the many tiny fishing settlements until the nineteenth century, it developed after the arrival of the railway. Jetties, fish-handling and freezing facilities sprang up to serve a growing fleet of trawlers and drifters, and the town became a ferry terminal of some importance for Skye and the smaller islands of the Inner Hebrides. It is a good centre too for exploring the mainland. There are splendid beaches, peaks, and Loch Morar – Britain's deepest freshwater loch – all within easy walking distance.

Cuillin Hills, Skye, Highland Region

Much of the magic of Scotland's western islands is centred in the Cuillin Hills, that stand above Soay Sound in Minginish, south-western Skye. Remote from the tourist routes, shrouded in mist (the less romantic call it drizzle), they were often the last that Victorian emigrants saw of the Hebrides when the sailing ships left for Nova Scotia and Newfoundland. Their heather-clad slopes still glow in the folk-memory of third and fourth generation Canadian Scots – MacLeods and Macdonalds, for whom the Cuillins are something to be seen on that long retirement trip to the old country. Nostalgic they may be, these damp green hills, but the living they offered to crofters and shepherds in the old days was never less than harsh. The brutalities of the Clearances that dispossessed the tenant farmers were in many ways attuned to the land itself. Perhaps the Cuillins are better left to the climbers and fell-walkers who enjoy them today. Despite their appearance of age, these are some of Britain's newest mountains, made up of lava and ash from Tertiary volcanoes.

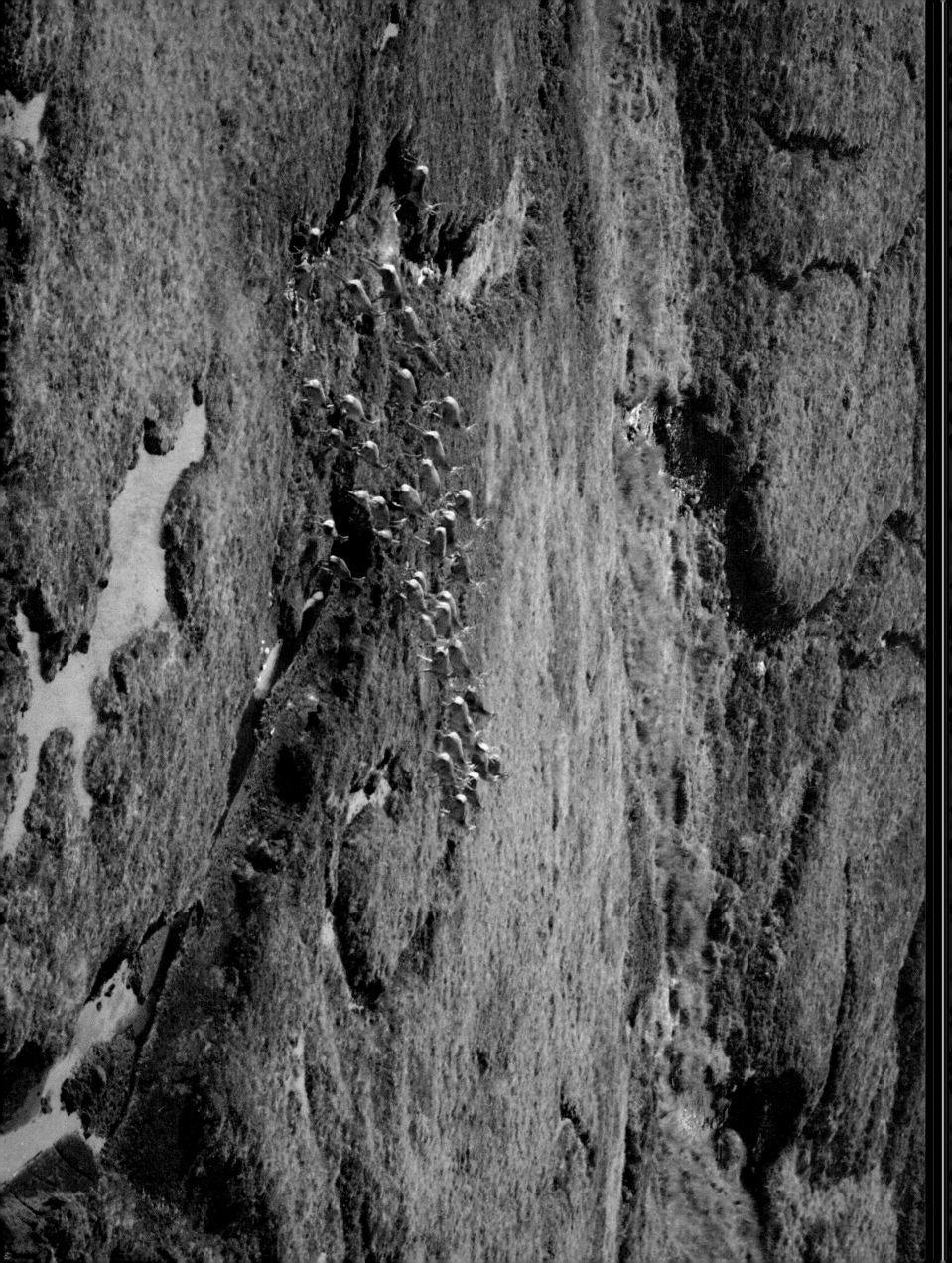

Deer, Highland Region

Red deer are traditional inhabitants of Britain, just as they are of the rest of northern Europe. In pre-industrial times they lived mainly in open forests and woodland, grazing in the glades during spring and summer, and browsing on trees and shrubs in winter. Over much of the country they were covered by forest law and could be hunted only by the king or those licensed by him. Today they are still quite common, though there is little forest left for them. They are not welcome in Forestry Commission plantations, where the aim is to grow tall, un-nibbled trees, so they tend to be found on open moorland, where they compete with sheep for the meagre growth. This is a less than optimal habitat for large browsing animals. Scottish deer are small compared with mainland European deer, and the descendants of British stocks exported to New Zealand in the nineteenth century are huge in comparison. Here a herd of young stags flees from the strange apparition in the sky. It is late September; their antlers are just about to mature and they are putting on heavy coats for the winter.

Strathpeffer, Highland Region

The north-west highlands of Scotland, crimped by crustal movements and scoured by glaciers, have taken on a strong east-west alignment. Blocks of ancient sandstones overlie an even older bedding of slates and schists, and both are cut by broad valleys that converge eastward to Cromarty Firth. Far north as they are, these are fertile valleys that repay cultivation and yield well under the long hours of summer sunshine. The Norse invaders prized them, later farmers have cherished them, and their small towns are comfortable, quiet places to live. Here we hover over Contin, with Loch Kinellan in the foreground, Loch Ussie in the right middle distance, and the little town of Strathpeffer nestling in the valley.

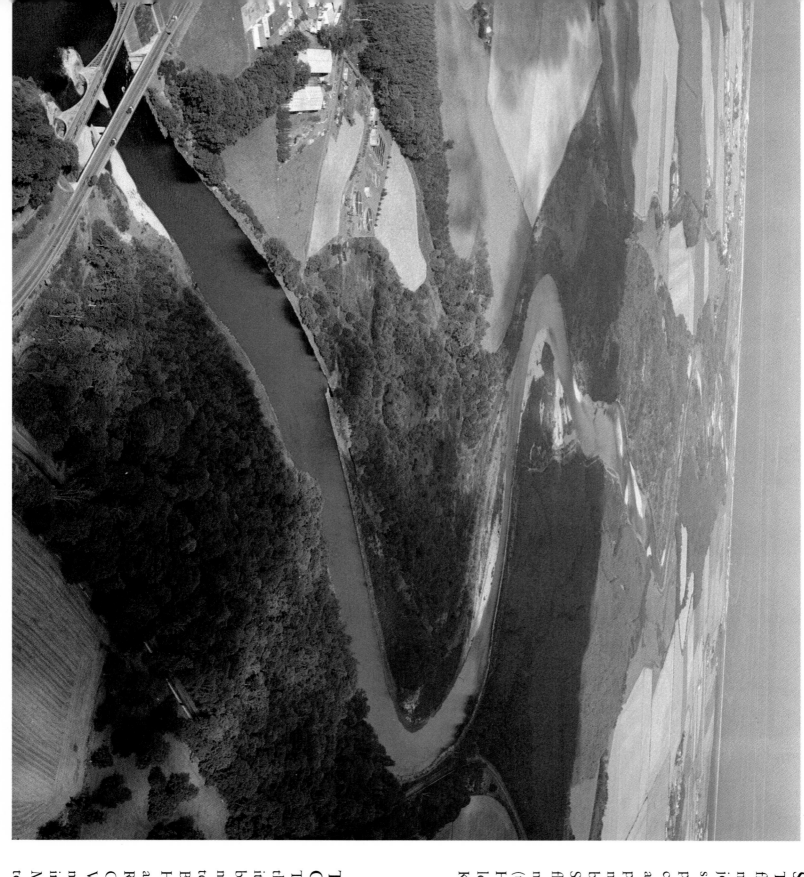

Strathspey, Grampian Region

The River Spey rises in the Corrieyairack Forest and flows north-eastward for more than 170 kilometres (105 miles) to its mouth on Moray Firth. Along the way it is joined by dozens of small tributaries, some from springs, some from heather moorlands, that between them provide a unique variety of waters. Mature salmon coming in from the sea scent the river far out in Spey Bay, and run upstream to find their home ground. At different points along the valley, the tributary waters are right for making the fierce golden liquid called Whisky. With barley for malting agleam in the sunny fields beside Strathspey, and peat to provide the subtle smokey flavour, no wonder the valley became a centre of whisky manufacture, with distilleries and bonded warehouses (that give time for ageing) at intervals along its length. Here we hover just over the bridges at Fochabers, looking north over the barley fields towards Garmouth, Kingston and Spey Bay.

The Dee Valley, near Braemar, Grampian Region

The Dee valley runs almost directly east and west, from the sources of the river on the flanks of the Cairngorms to its mouth at Aberdeen. From Braemar eastward it is a broad valley, scenic and relatively unspoiled, with a meandering but purposeful river continuing the long-term business of shaping it. Well into the Highlands, Braemar is the site of the Royal Highland Gathering. Held every September, this is a festival of dancing, games and tossing cabers, often under the patronage of the Royal Family who stay just down the road at Balmoral Castle. The royal connection began with Queen Victoria, whose visits to the Highlands and concern for matters north of the Border did much to revive a general interest in things Scottish. If it also began the McHaggisry that fills the tourist shops of Princes Street today, who but the Scots themselves can complain.

Stirling University, Stirling, Central Region

The geological faults that cross central Scotland from east to west provide a sharp limit to the central plain. Here on a fault line stands Stirling, once the seat of the Kings of Scotland, and one of the many centres that tour-operators like to call The Gateway to the Highlands. Stirling is an ancient town, clustered about its castle on the banks of the Forth. Bannockburn and half a dozen other major battles were fought within sight of its walls during Scotland's struggles with her unruly English neighbours. Now Stirling is a peaceful, seemly burgh that has recently acquired a bustling new university. Here is the university, in its lakeside campus five kilometres (three miles) from the centre of town. Beyond it lie Alloa and the broad plain of the Central Lowlands; behind it rise the slopes of Dumyat (418 metres, 1,371 feet) and the Ochil Hills.

Firth of Forth, Lothian Region

Too wide to bridge at Edinburgh itself, the Firth of Forth was for long a barrier that diverted traffic and interest westward through Falkirk and Stirling. However the east coast rail-route needed a bridge as far to the east as possible, and the narrowest crossing – Queensferry – was chosen. Designer Benjamin Baker built strong. Using the rocky islet of Inch Garvie as a stepping stone he threw three linked cantilevers of steel across the Firth: here we see two of them. It took almost sixty thousand tonnes of steel, and they've been painting it ever since to keep steel and sea air apart. Baker's Forth Bridge solved the railway problem, but road traffic still had to go round by Kincardine. So in the late 1950s they began building again, this time the delicate suspension bridge that carries roadways, footpaths and cycle-tracks across. Brute strength and elegance cross the Firth together, and there is an intriguing harmony between them. Both bridges are in view as we look west toward Grangemouth and Stirling.

Edinburgh, Lothian Region

Edinburgh took its name from Edwin, the Saxon king of
Northumbria who held it in the seventh century. Its
unofficial name – Auld Reekie – tells of the smoke pall
that hung over the growing city from the seventeenth
century onward. Edinburgh's history is turbulent,
starting well before Edwin. Castle Rock (centre right)
was fortified in prehistoric times – Romans, Britons and
Picts in turn clustered under its protection. In medieval
times castle and Old Town (beyond it to the left) grew up
together under the mound of Arthur's Seat (background). Edinburgh was then a strongly walled city of
tall houses and narrow wynds, ringed by protective crags
and perched on the northern frontier of civilization. In
the late eighteenth century, with Jacobites subdued, the
city broke from its cocoon and spread. Bridges spanned
the gulf that hemmed it in to the north, and a splendid
New Town of Georgian streets, squares and crescents
(foreground, and inset) took shape on the open ground
beyond. Edinburgh's grace and success as a place for
living owe much to the New Town concept. Scotsmen
seem to agree; after havering between Scone, Perth and
Stirling they finally made Edinburgh their capital, and
now one in ten of them lives here.

Hawick, Borders Region

'Hawick has a romantic situation' wrote traveller William Gilpin in 1776, 'among rocks, sounding rivers, cataracts and bridges; all of which are very picturesque'. Largest of the Border towns, Hawick stands only 20 kilometres (twelve miles) from England on the slopes of the Cheviot Hills, where Slitrig Water joins the Teviot. During the fifteenth and sixteenth centuries it made easy prey for English raiding parties; they burned it down twice in the sixteenth century, eventually leaving only the Baron's Tower standing. Not surprisingly, it is short of ancient buildings. Hawick picked itself up after each attack, and continued in its role of market town for a large and rich sheep farming area. In the eighteenth century it took to knitting. 1771 saw the introduction into Hawick of the first stocking frames in Scotland and the town expanded as an industrial knitwear centre. Fine Scottish woollens have a lasting appeal, and Hawick's prosperity is still based on its skills in handling wool. Here some of the tall tenement buildings near the centre of the town huddle to talk over times past.

Farne Islands, Northumberland

They lie off Bamburgh, some 30 of them at low tide, ranging from sea-worn stacks to islands of several hectares. Remote and relatively inaccessible, the Farnes were much favoured by hermit monks in medieval times. Birds love their basalt columns and ledges. They are a nesting place for eider ducks, puffins and kittiwakes, and a stepping-off place for thousands of migrants that move up and down the coast in spring and autumn. Seals too love the Farnes. There is a flourishing colony of breeding grey seals – too flourishing for the local fishermen, who claim that they eat the salmon. Here we look south-west across the Farne Islands from Longstone toward the Northumberland coast. Inner Farne, the largest island, is in the far distance; Brownsman is the long island in the middle distance. It was from the Longstone Lighthouse in 1838 that Grace Darling and her father rowed to Big Hardcar Rock (the round, split reef in the middle distance) to rescue survivors from a wrecked steamer.

North Seaton, Northumberland

The industrial north-east is built on coal, and there are pits with winding-gear, railway sidings, spoil-tips and general ugliness all the way along this stretch of the North Sea coast. From local ports the coal was shipped by keels and coasters to London and across the North Sea. Here rich seams dip eastward beyond the shore and coal may be mined as far as six kilometres (nearly four miles) out under the sea. The coast itself remains relatively unspoilt by the impact of mining. There are only a few resorts and their tradition has not, on the whole, included large-scale family accommodation. Hence this and many similar caravan parks along the cliff-tops, which cater for hundreds of miners and industrial workers on weekends and summer vacations. North Seaton lies just along the road, and the town of Ashington (p. 100) is only a few miles inland from here.

Ashington, Northumberland

Up in Northumbria they take their coal mining seriously. This is Ashington, a town built in Victorian times and virtually dedicated to its pits and the miners who work them. These are traditional Victorian terraced houses, not the best of their kind but far from the worst, put up to accommodate the miners and their families who flocked in when the new pits were opened during the mid-to-late nineteenth century. So arose a town that lives – and one day might die – by coal. So far it has been lucky. The once flourishing overseas trade has gone, but Ashington continues to mine coal to meet the insatiable demands of local power stations. In its spare time it plays football. Bobby Charlton was born here, and many other fine footballers have learned their art in this part of the world.

Housesteads, Northumberland

Just over 2,000 years ago, in the time of the Emperor Hadrian, an army of swarthy soldiers marched up to north Britain. Today we would call them Italians. History calls them Romans, but they seem to have been a mixed bunch from all over central and southern Europe – Hadrian himself was a Spaniard. By one means or another they persuaded the local people to build a wall some five metres (15 feet) high, 120 kilometres (73 miles) long and peppered with garrisons, to keep out the northerners. It can be seen emerging from the trees in the bottom left hand corner, and winding away from us (eastward) along the left hand side of the fort and beyond. If the locals resented this extraordinary imposition, the sight of their Mediterranean masters turning blue with cold on sentry-go must have cheered them considerably. This central section of the wall was built along the Whin Sill, a ridge of hard intruded dolerite that outcrops among the local limestones, providing a raised foundation. The fort is Housesteads, one of 16 small, stone-built garrisons with accommodation for about 1,000 troops and some at least of their camp followers. It was probably administered from Vindolanda, a much larger base a few kilometres to the south.

Washington, Tyne and Wear

The industrial North-East, centred about the River Tyne, owes its former prosperity to minerals, notably coal, iron, and the salt that formed the basis of its chemical industries. Shipbuilding and many other industries followed. These were mostly village-sized operations, but now times have changed. It is said that small-scale operations are no longer economical, and pits, factories, shipyards and workshops have closed, leaving whole villages on the dole. One answer is the creation of new towns – whole communities planned from the start, with new industries, housing and amenities to attract families from semi-derelict villages and old towns. This is Washington, just a few kilometres south of Gateshead. A mining village of that name was flattened to provide the site. Only the Old Hall remains, dimly connected with the family of George Washington and much restored with American funds. Can the New Town concept work? In the North-East people are proud of their roots and fiercely independent. If it can work here, it can work anywhere.

Durham, County Durham

Another city built in the protective bend of a river – another reminder of the civil strife that plagued Britain in early medieval times. The river is the Wear, the site a sandstone bluff. The builders were the Normans, and the enemy were the Scots, against whom the castle and protective wall blocked the neck of the peninsula. The castle was for the incumbent prince-bishop, responsible for defence as well as the cure of souls. Durham Cathedral, built to replace an earlier shrine for the remains of St Cuthbert, was begun in 1093. With its squat pillars and soaring arches it is arguably the foremost Norman building in Britain, if not in Europe. Not surprisingly, Durham developed mainly as an ecclesiastical city and centre of learning. The University, founded in 1832, is England's third oldest after Oxford and Cambridge; however, it was long preceded by a divinity school dating back to the fifteenth century. Well established as a county administrative centre, Durham has managed to fend off the grosser forms of industry and acquire a medieval charm that could never have existed in rude medieval times.

Whitby, North Yorkshire

Here the River Esk has cut a steep valley through limestone cliffs, and broadened to form a harbour – one of the few natural havens along this section of the Yorkshire coastline. Whitby began with first a Celtic and later a Benedictine monastery on the south-eastern clifftops, developing as a port for fishing and ship-building. Captain James Cook, a local lad, chose a Whitby-built collier to take him around the world in the 1770s, and Whitby whalers sailed north to penetrate the Greenland pack-ice in search of their prey during the nineteenth century. Whitby is still a fishing port, centred upon its little harbour at the mouth of the Esk, and still has many fine Georgian and early Victorian buildings to remind it of its past. Now it is also a holiday resort. That little church on the clifftop in the bottom right hand corner is worth noting. Originally Norman, it was partly rebuilt in Georgian times by carpenters trained in shipbuilding; its box-pews, three-tiered pulpit and high windows all have a touch of the sailing ship about them.

Fountains Abbey, North Yorkshire

In 1132 thirteen dissenting monks left the Benedictine abbey of St Mary's at York to set up their own establishment under Cistercian rule near Ripon. They chose a wild site in the valley of the River Skell, where water welled from the limestone rock; there they founded what was to become one of the wealthiest religious communities in Britain – Fountains Abbey. Fountains owed its wealth to benefactors who gave the community land, both locally and across the north of England, for the production of wool. By the end of the thirteenth century Fountains was the most important wool producer in north Britain, and the abbey itself, virtually complete, was among the finest and largest in the land. So it continued till 1539, when its wealth was surrendered to the king. A year later its dismantling had begun, and the ruin we see today dates from that time. Parts of it were used to build nearby Fountains Hall (foreground). Fountains Abbey holds a magic that no guide book can describe and no photograph express. Visit it on a fine summer evening when the crowds have gone, and you'll see what I mean.

York, North Yorkshire

It was an important Roman settlement on the River Ouse, and in Anglo-Saxon times became the Northumbrian capital. The Danes took it over in 867 and stayed 100 years. They called it Jorvik, and the foundations of their little port and market town, now re-exposed, form one of York's many tourist attractions. The Normans in time created a walled town. Their walls, bordered with daffodils in spring, today form an irregular ring about the medieval heart of the city, centred on the huge thirteenth-to-fifteenth-century Minster. Though far from the sea, York was an important port throughout the Middle Ages; most winters the Ouse floods houses and cellars along its banks, to remind the city of its long-standing debt. Wool

and agricultural produce from the fertile Vale of York were its mainstays. Then the railways brought engineering and other industries, and York spread and diversified. Most of its industries developed, thank heaven, outside the walls, so the inner town remains almost intact. Here we see the city from the south, dominated by the Minster (centre, and inset). The medieval huddle of buildings about the Minster, especially within the walls, contrasts with the orderly rows of industrial housing on the outskirts of the city.

Headingley, Leeds, West Yorkshire

Not every suburb of a northern industrial town is as well laid-out as this one. With its housing developments that span the century, its mature trees and gardens, its range of styles from Edwardian villa to high-rise flat, it could be a remarkably pleasant corner for a northern Everyman to live. To appreciate it fully, however, he would need to be both a Yorkshireman and a cricket enthusiast. For this is the Leeds suburb of Headingley and there in the middle is the shrine of northern cricket – the sacred ground of the Yorkshire County Cricket Club. There's a match on and it looks like a big one, with a capacity crowd of 15,000 to 18,000 and extra parking on the rugby pitch next door. That's an interesting line-up of fielders in the slips – if cricketers wore striped shirts, we could tell who was playing Yorkshire.

Ferrybridge, West Yorkshire

Follow the line of the Humber inland toward the Pennines and you cross a plain of low-lying farmland dotted with colliery towns. On the surface they grow wheat, oats and fields full of red-stemmed rhubarb; below the rolling ground is one of the world's richest coalfields, mined now for several centuries and still likely to yield in abundance for centuries more. Here we move eastward in the direction of Goole, following the M62 motorway as it winds between Castleford (lower left) and the northern outskirts of Pontefract (lower right). The road that crosses the motorway at the clover-leaf junction is the A1, for long Britain's main highway north and still an important trunk-road. The huge power station with its eight cooling towers is Ferrybridge, fed by local coal and named after the small village alongside. The pillar of vapour beyond represents Eggborough, and the one beyond that Drax – power stations that draw on the same coalfield.

Kingston-upon-Hull, Humberside

Kingston-upon-Hull grew up where the muddy River Hull joins the even muddier Humber Estuary, developing by stages into a city of more than 300,000 inhabitants. Its citizens roll includes Andrew Marvell, William Wilberforce, Amy Johnson and Ian Carmichael. One of the few deep-water ports of north-eastern England, its medieval moat became a ring of docks that reached into the heart of the city, and Hull plied a lively trade with continental neighbours. The home, too, of deep-water trawlers that ventured north to Greenland and the White Sea, in the inter-war years it became Britain's first fishing port. Then Hull's tide of prosperity turned. The innermost of its dock basins, Queen's Dock, was filled in to become a decorative garden (centre) still flanked in part by Victorian warehouses, and supervised by Wilberforce on his column (lower end). Much of the city centre had to be rebuilt after World War II bombing. Now the trawler fleet and much of the shipping trade have disappeared, and Hull is no longer the city it was. Perhaps the new Humber Bridge, just a few miles up-river, will help to bring it back into circulation.

Grimsby, Humberside

Sail up the Humber Estuary and Grimsby is the first
haven you come to – a small town on a low, sandy shore,
with extensive docks and fish-processing factories.
Though there is not much to show for it, Grimsby dates
from pre-Conquest days when the Danes ruled the
North-East. Grim was a fisherman who saved Havelock,
an exiled prince, from drowning. When Havelock
became king he rewarded Grim with land and capital for
a harbour. The town remained a small fishing haven
until the mid-nineteenth century. Then the railways
came, new docks were built, and Grimsby became an
important fishing centre with its own fleet of trawlers,
and a port for handling coastal trade, especially with
Scandinavia. Like Kingston-upon-Hull, its larger rival
across the estuary, Grimsby was hard-hit when Icelandic
and other distant waters were closed to British trawlers.
Now the docks are modernized for container traffic, and
are still busy with cargoes to and from Norway,
Denmark and Sweden, and fish is still bought for
processing from foreign vessels. And Grimsby has its
own special fleet of seiners – small fishing boats that net
surface shoals in the North Sea. Here is a group of mixed
Grimsby boats, lined up at the harbour wall for
revictualling, like cattle at a trough.

Mablethorpe, Lincolnshire

Camels crossing the Sahara? No – just a string of horses
exercising on a Lincolnshire beach close to the resort of
Mablethorpe.

Skegness, Lincolnshire

Much of the low-lying Lincolnshire coast has to be protected from erosion, with costly concrete ramparts and wooden groynes that help to stabilize the beaches. The sea just roars and rolls off; with time on its side, it can afford to. By a quirk of fate Skegness has no such problem. Its hectares of sandy shore give little trouble, and the town has sensibly put a long, broad promenade with boating lakes and floral gardens between itself and the enemy. This is another little village that the Victorian railway planners touched and brought prosperity to – a splendid coastal resort that pleases thousands of visitors every year.

The Wash, Lincolnshire

The Witham, Welland, Nene and Great Ouse are four soupy rivers that carry mud from the fenlands into the Wash. Hitting salt water, the thin mud settles, forming huge, shifting banks that line the land and merge with the sea. Slowly, the land is spreading. Man speeds up the process with a drainage scheme here, a sea wall there, and to very good effect; the shore where King John lost his baggage train is now six to eight kilometres (four to five miles) inland and well cultivated. But the Wash is filling up gradually anyway. Let us not be in too much of a hurry to help, for muddy shores and shallows have a lot to be said for them – if not by man, by birds. The thousands upon thousands of migrant ducks, geese, swans and shorebirds that pour into the Wash every year and feed on the pickings of the rich mud would find turnip fields a poor exchange – and so would the thousands of bird lovers who come to enjoy their company.

Boston, Lincolnshire

Anglo-Saxon monk St Botolph seems to have spread his influence widely. There are churches up and down the country dedicated to him; Boston's is perhaps the largest and most famous, and the town owes its name to him too. Boston's origins are uncertain, but it was already a flourishing port in the thirteenth century. The church is mainly fourteenth-century, and the splendid tower with its eight-sided lantern was completed in 1460. The 'Stump' is a landmark that landsmen must have appreciated as much as mariners in the early days. Boston fell on hard times in the seventeenth century when the channel of the River Witham silted up and competition from other ports grew. Now it flourishes again. It is a place of special interest for Americans, for some of the Pilgrim Fathers sailed from Boston in 1608. Reaching New England after a long stay in the Netherlands, they founded its counterpart in Massachusetts in 1630.

114

Weston, near Spalding, Lincolnshire

South Lincolnshire and the land around it should not be there at all. By rights they should be salt-marsh, fen, or part of the sea bed in a much more extensive Wash. Holland is the name of the area about Spalding; like its namesake across the North Sea it is mostly low-lying, and criss-crossed with dykes and canals. Generations of patient draining and delving have rescued the land, cleansed its fertile soils and turned them over to production. Cereals and vegetables are the main crops, but these are tulip fields, flushed with spring colour. Travellers who take package trips to the Netherlands at tulip-time might be pleasantly surprised by Spalding, which now manages its own tulip festival every May.

Belvoir, Lincolnshire

There is a small, attractive village, an extraordinary castle belonging to the Dukes of Rutland, and a gentle vale, all called Belvoir. 'Belvedere' was the original name, and a beautiful view there is too across the vale. The good folk of Rutland shortened it, and shortened it yet again by pronouncing it 'Beever'. Belvoir lies just west of Grantham off the A1. There is nothing especially remarkable about it – just another lovely corner of Britain that man has developed for agriculture and made curiously satisfying. There's a canal running through the heart of it, built long ago and now fully integrated, and a network of roads that take nothing from its beauty. Belvoir however is threatened, because a huge coalfield, possibly Europe's biggest reserve, has been discovered deep beneath it. Developers want to sink three mines, two within eight kilometres (five miles) of the village, and the third within 16 kilometres (10 miles). There will be spoil tips, railways, and housing for about 5,000 miners and their families, mostly to the west of what we see here. If it happens, it will be a long time before the vale becomes its peaceful self again.

Sheffield, South Yorkshire

A huge city of more than half a million people, sprawled over hillsides and dedicated to heavy industry, isn't likely to be everybody's favourite resort. However, Sheffield's late-nineteenth and early-twentieth-century awfulness has been mitigated – replaced, some would say, by a new awfulness, though that is not what the people of Sheffield seem to think. As the old geography books used to tell us, Sheffield's prosperity was founded on sharp-edged steel. Iron-stone, limestone and water-power were present in abundance to make the steel, with the additional component – graded gritstones – to provide the sharpening. Sheffield developed a monopoly in cutlery, suffering inevitably when other countries discovered how to produce it more cheaply. However, the city had other irons in its fire as well, including type-founding, iron and stainless steel production, and dozens of smaller industries. Partly destroyed during World War II, it has rehoused huge sections of its population on modern housing estates on the slopes overlooking the city. Here is part of the elegant Norfolk Park development, built in the 1960s only four kilometres (two and a half miles) south-east of the city centre.

Chesterfield, Derbyshire

South from Sheffield the Pennines give way to rolling country threaded by rivers and dotted with small, semi-industrial towns. There is coal in abundance under most of it, but not always easy to work. These small towns have not committed themselves to industry and grime quite as compulsively as Sheffield in the north or Derby, Nottingham and Leicester to the south. They live more by their wits. Some, like Matlock, retain the image of a spa-town in a beautiful setting, others have light industry and small-scale manufacturing as their mainstay. Chesterfield is just such a town – undistinguished to outsiders but comfortable to those who know it, with a history going back to Roman times and beyond. It has a church of distinction, built in the fourteenth century and still going strong, but so much a part of everyday life that it is practically ignored. Or it would be but for the twisted spire. Because of some quirk in the timber the parish church of St Mary and All Saints, Chesterfield, has for 600 years worn its spire rakishly, well over one eye – and a plague on anyone who ever tries to put it straight.

Donington Park, Leicestershire

Donington Park, near Castle Donington, is open for diversions of various kinds. There is a race-track and an automobile museum, and here is an Event – perhaps a pop-festival, a down-market Glyndebourne – or the annual meeting of the Society for the Promotion of Queuing. It is worth using a hand-lens on this one, to see what capers our species gets up to when gathered together by the thousand.

Gravelly Hill, Birmingham, West Midlands

During the mid-nineteenth century a network of railways was flung across the face of Britain. Iron rails snaked through forests and parklands, bridged rivers and estuaries, crossed moss, moorland and pasture, parting towns from their suburbs and farmers from their fields. They were cheered by progressives as the route to the future and bewailed by conservatives who liked Britain the way it was. Now the future is with us and motorways are doing much the same thing. Egged on by lobbies of road-users and by the decline in railways and canals, the planners have drawn up a new network of concrete highways that, like the railways before them, slash disruptive straight lines through a countryside of curves. But – again like the railways – motorways have their own beauty and elegance. Here at Spaghetti Junction (the bureaucrats call it Gravelly Hill Interchange) the M6, the A38 and the A5127 meet in the north-eastern suburbs of Birmingham. They tangle, embrace, and spawn a welter of slip-roads that race off in all directions on concrete stilts. There is a canal junction and a railway line involved as well. Fun for the planners, fun for the motorists and lorry drivers, fun for the civil engineers and contractors who spread the spaghetti – it's fun for almost everyone. Not, perhaps, fun for the folk who live down there beyond the A38. Bemused by the noise and the fumes, they'll be wondering wryly what happened to all those splendid Victorian railway lines.

Leicester, Leicestershire

The Romans began Leicester when they built the substantial township of Ratae Coritanorum where their Fosse Way crossed the River Soar. After they left the town continued to grow. There were over 300 good houses recorded in Leicester in the Domesday Book, with an Anglo-Saxon church and a castle planned and partly built. There were Bishops of Leicester in the eighth century AD, and a modern Leicester infant can, if desired, be christened at a font where baptisms have been carried out for over seven centuries. Hosiery and knitwear, boots and shoes were its stock-in-trade in the past, but today engineering is taking over from them. Here we hover over the southern end of the city and look north towards the cathedral (upper left) with a cluster of old red-brick buildings about it. In the foreground King Street and Welford Road converge slightly toward the interlocking commas of the City Council's new offices.

Corby, Northamptonshire

Here at the northern end of Northamptonshire, in the triangle between Leicester, Peterborough and Northampton itself, lies the once-green area of Rockingham Forest. Over the years the trees have been cut for timber, fuel, and tanbark for the local leather industry, leaving the land clear for agriculture and building. However, it has remained an attractive area, fields alternating with woodlands and villages in a pattern we have come to regard as traditional and very, very English. For this section of Rockingham Forest the pattern changed more drastically. Corby has long been associated with iron smelting (it was mentioned as such in the Domesday survey), for the Jurassic limestones underlying it are rich in iron ores. Its huge iron and steel complex was built in 1933, and in 1950 it became a New Town, with a projected population of 82,000. Here on the outskirts of town the iron-stone is being lifted by open-cast quarrying — or so it was until the end of 1979 when steel production at Corby came to an end. Tube and pipe manufacture continues, but the New Town is looking hard for new industries to replace the old one it has lost.

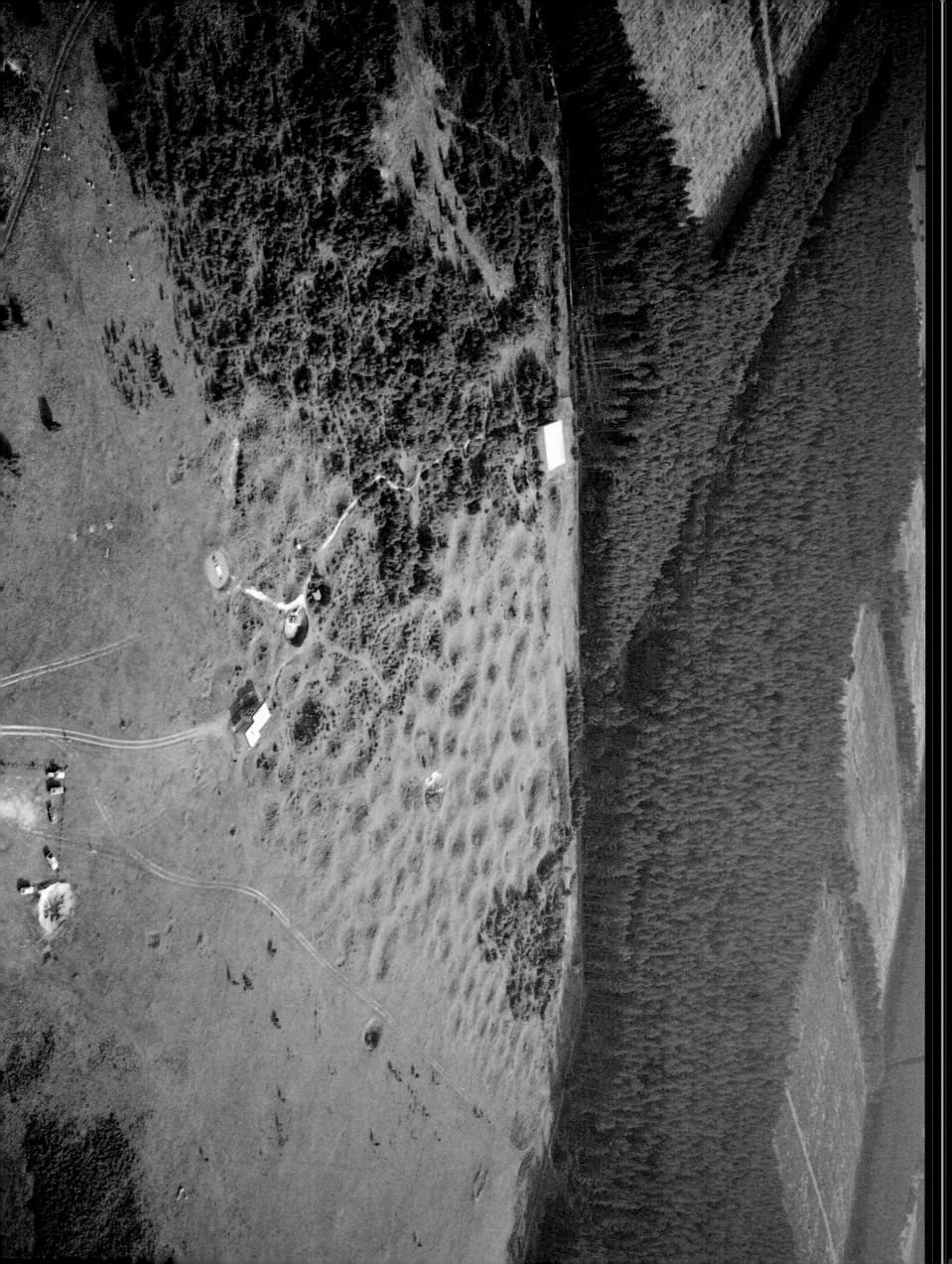

Grime's Graves, Norfolk

One of Britain's earliest industrial sites, this area of grassy mounds and hollows lies between Mundford and Santon Downham on the Norfolk-Suffolk border. The mounds, some 4,000 years old, are spoil heaps. The pits are long-filled shafts dug through the underlying chalk to depths of seven metres (23 feet) or more in search of flints – nodules of silica that grew in warm chalk seas and accumulated in layers. To Stone Age man flint was a godsend – by far the hardest substance he had to deal with, capable of being chipped to form keen-edged knives, sickles, axes and arrowheads. Many were knapped (shaped) on the spot and then exported far and wide across Britain. The pits were ascribed to Grime or Grim (alternative names for the Norse god Woden) by later generations, along with other inexplicable dykes and earthworks. They are long disused, but flint-knapping for building stones continues in some of the neighbouring villages.

Norwich, Norfolk

Here is a city that has worked well for more than 1,000 years, and looks all set for at least 1,000 more. It began as an Anglo-Saxon town in a loop of the River Wensum and was growing nicely when the Danes sailed up and sacked it in 1004. The cathedral, begun shortly after the Conquest, is one of the finest Norman buildings in England, with the largest cloisters. The castle keep dates from the same period: for long a gaol, it is now an excellent museum. The two stand in the walled heart of the city with many other fine buildings alongside. Norwich is a focal point for East Anglia, and has attracted immigrants – Jews, Flemish protestant weavers and many others – who brought their skills and made it a prosperous community. The Industrial Revolution by-passed it, Norwich had no reserves of fuel or raw materials to draw on. But it kept its head and developed light engineering, boot and shoe manufacture, and almost cornered the market in mustard, chocolate and other foodstuffs.

The Broads, Norfolk

Between Norwich and the coast of Norfolk, from Hickling in the north to Lowestoft in the south, lies a lowland triangle of meandering, aimless rivers, dotted with lakes, tarns and marshes. There is enough firm ground for roads and railways, fields and villages too, but the Broads are obviously an area where water is an important factor. A boat may not be essential for business-as-usual, but must obviously be handy. The Broads are in fact largely man-made, by generations of turf-cutters who sold their acid, peaty topsoil for fuel. The rivers have obligingly filled the gaps. The Broads could be drained without too much difficulty and turned into agricultural land. But hands up those who want marshes or agricultural land, and hands up those who want things kept as they are for lazy boating and birdwatching? The thousands of visitors have it, and the Broads will be kept broad for as a long as possible with dredging, weed-cutting and clearing. Here the River Bure winds below us from Hoveton and Wroxham villages (top left) past Wroxham, Hoveton Great and Salhouse Broads.

Great Yarmouth, Norfolk

Great Yarmouth is built on a spit of land that has extended southward since AD 400, almost but not quite bottling up the estuary – Breydon Water – that drains several of the Broads. Great Yarmouth was a landing point for the Romans, and a herring fishing port for those who came later. In the fourteenth century it was walled. Rows of tightly-packed houses still exist in the inner town. The people of Great Yarmouth have taken every possible advantage of its splendid situation, developing their sheltered estuary as a port, with about seven kilometres (four miles) of quays for North Sea trading and the servicing of oil and gas rigs. The outer coast is for fun: there is a wide beach, and everything the visitor needs to keep him entertained on a sunny afternoon.

Aldeburgh, Suffolk

Here on the south-eastern coast of Suffolk the sea seems intent on shifting everything southward; from Dunwich to Aldeburgh the shore is receding, beyond Orford Ness to the south-west it is building up. It would be a pity if Aldeburgh disappeared, as neighbouring Slaughden did in the early years of this century, for it is a pleasant little town, with an annual music festival second to none. It was one of the small coastal fishing villages that prospered throughout the nineteenth century on herring. Nowadays its fishing has declined, but Aldeburgh has become a quiet seaside resort, noted for its biting fresh air. There is little to see except the sixteenth-century church on the hill, an Elizabethan Moot Hall standing precariously by the shore, and rows of small sturdy houses that face the sea bravely. There is plenty however to hear in June, when musicians gather to honour music and the memory of Benjamin Britten, who helped to found the festival in 1948.

Orford Ness, Suffolk

Orford Ness forms a turning point along the low Suffolk coast. Behind it lie a blind channel and the River Alde, that separate the Ness from the mainland. In medieval times the shingle spit reached little further south than the village of Orford. Since then it has lengthened by about eight kilometres (five miles), excluding Orford from access to the sea except by the River Ore, the southward extension of the Alde. Within the Ore lies Havergate Island, a low shingle ridge famous for its spring colonies of breeding birds. Most famous of all visitors is the avocet, a shore-bird rare in Britain that has been breeding there since 1947. Orford stands in the bend of the river (top left), with the north end of Havergate Island below; on the right overlapping patterns of shingle sweep up toward the lighthouse (top right) and on round the corner to Aldeburgh.

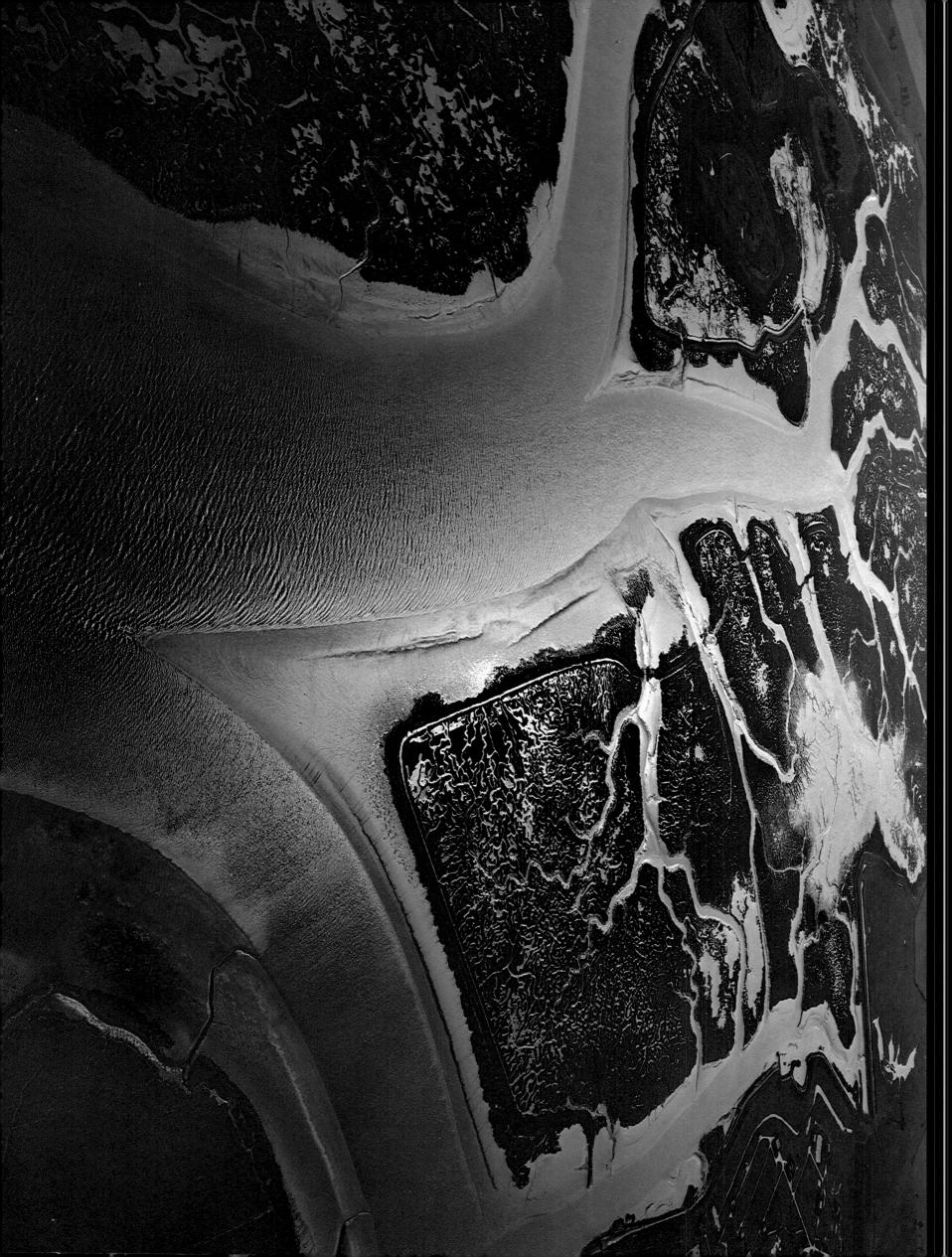

Hamford Water, Essex

Perhaps one of the remotest corners of Britain, this huge mudflat lies in the deep embayment between Harwich and Walton on the Naze, stretching south-westward in the direction of Beaumont and Thorpe-le-Soken. A drowned river valley with low, marshy islands, it is barely accessible by road and treacherous for walkers. Yachtsmen are happy to use it as a refuge and can tie up at tiny, long-forgotten jetties – but there are few shore facilities for them. Here we look up Hamford Water with Horsey and Skipper's Islands on the left. Discerning ducks, geese and waders favour it as a winter refuge and spring breeding-ground, and long may it stay that way.

Wivenhoe, Essex

Wivenhoe is a small waterside township at the head of the Colne estuary, south-east of Colchester, with a muddy foreshore and a quay for small cargo boats. There are boatyards with slipways where new ships could be built, except that they are too busy repairing old ones. These are traditional Essex houses built of whatever has come to hand – bricks, clay, timber, perhaps even driftwood. Some are nicely pargeted – faced with beautifully-patterned plasterwork. There's a decent church; the tower is fifteenth-century, and the rest might have been too but for an earthquake, of all things, about a century ago. That was in Wivenhoe's hey-day, when the large sea-going yachts of the gentry used to be hauled up for their winter refurbishing. Now it is usually smaller craft that are serviced. The further you get from the quay at Wivenhoe the less traditional and the more red-brick it becomes, housing different kinds of people unconnected with the river. Further away still is Essex University with its grey skyscraper towers. How they are supposed to link in with a nice old river port is hard to imagine.

Cambridge, Cambridgeshire

East Anglia's most distinguished city, Cambridge was once a Celtic settlement on a low hill by the river Cam. The Romans settled by a ford and later built a bridge. In the centuries that followed Cambridge developed into a small market town on the southern edge of the Fens. In medieval times, like many other such towns, it attracted monastic scholars. Several came from Oxford to Cambridge during the early thirteenth century, and in 1231 Henry III declared Cambridge a centre of learning – effectively founding the university. The first college, Peterhouse, was established in 1284, and over a dozen others had come into being by the end of the sixteenth century. Their buildings – chapels, houses and halls of residence – dominate the centre of the city and river bank, contributing largely to the fusty charm that visitors love. A few, like King's College Chapel (seen here slightly right of centre), are truly elegant both inside and out, from the ground and from the air. Here we drift over The Backs – the riverside walk behind the colleges. It is a good vantage point for seeing both the collegiate centre of the city and some of the industrial and residential suburbs surrounding it.

Ridgmont, Bedfordshire

Per passenger per mile, motorways are safer by far than lesser roads. They are faster, more convenient and less wearing to drive on than almost anything they have replaced. 'Motorways are safe', say their champions. 'It's drivers who are dangerous.' They are probably right at that. This pile-up occurred on a mid-March day, in poor visibility at the junction of the M1 and the A5140. Motorway police and nearby hospitals were ready for it – March fogs bring accidents as surely as April rain brings flowers. There were deaths and disablements; many will remember the event with horror. It was fortunate that the safety barrier held – the really nasty accidents are the ones involving both streams of traffic.

Milton Keynes, Buckinghamshire

In the northern corner of Buckinghamshire, not far from the MI motorway, the largest of all Britain's New Towns is developing. Until 1967 Milton Keynes was a tiny village on the River Ouzel, then it began to spread. It is planned to engulf the neighbouring towns of Wolverton, Bletchley and Stony Stratford, and may grow to a city of 200,000 by the end of the century. Only a few cottages and a church remain of the original village, almost lost in the rash of new housing and industrial estates; some of the hedgelines can still be seen. Milton Keynes has proved popular. Close enough to London to attract both modern industry and commuters, it has all the makings of a boom town. Low buildings, pleasant layouts and a neighbourhood concept of housing augur well for the future. Perhaps we are learning at last from the urban planning disasters of post-war years.

Deanshanger, Northamptonshire
Weak sunlight and lowering, snow-filled clouds – a typical late-winter scene over the English Midlands. Once a tiny inland port on a branch of the Grand Union Canal, Deanshanger lays a scaled-down smoke pall from its works' chimneys. The mosaic of empty fields, snow-powdered, hedged with hawthorn, ash and elm, waits in silence for the better times that are bound to come.

Stratford-upon-Avon, Warwickshire

The Upper Avon winds gently through western Warwickshire. Here, where it was shallow enough to ford, the Romans built a staging post that grew into a market town. By medieval times it was prosperous and in 1553 it received its charter. Eleven years later, William Shakespeare, Stratford's most distinguished son, was born in a half-timbered house that still stands in Henley Street. The small community could not hold a budding playwright and actor for long. After marrying a local girl and starting a family of his own, Shakespeare left for London, returning from time to time to enjoy some of the comforts of his growing income. He died at Stratford in 1616, and is buried here in Holy Trinity Church. Bardolatry – the cult of Shakespeare – began in the mid-eighteenth century when actor David Garrick held a festival of his plays there. The Memorial Theatre, built in 1879, was destroyed by fire and rebuilt in 1932. Now Stratford-upon-Avon, still a delightful market town, is Britain's greatest tourist attraction outside London. Here we drift north along the Avon. The theatre, now called the Royal Shakespeare Theatre, is on the left bank of the river just before the bridges.

King's Sutton, Northamptonshire

From the air Britain is an ever-changing patchwork of colour. There are the many different shades of soil – rich black in the fens, red in the West Country, sandy in the Midlands, white-flecked on the chalk downs. There are also the colours of the crops, from the pale green of growing wheat to the ever-spreading yellow of oilseed rape. Identifying crops and judging their performances is one of the many interests a light-aircraft pilot or balloonist can cultivate on cross-country flights. Here between Banbury and Aynho, where Oxfordshire and Northampton meet, we hover over an unusual patch of colour – a field of crimson clover in full bloom.

Blenheim Palace, Woodstock, Oxfordshire

For his victories in the War of the Spanish Succession, notably at the Battle of Blenheim, John Churchill, Duke of Marlborough, was given the Royal Manor of Woodstock by a grateful Queen Anne. Not to be outdone, Parliament voted him a huge sum of spending money which the first Duke put toward a palace. He commissioned Sir John Vanbrugh who had just finished Castle Howard, and the foundation stone of Blenheim Palace was laid in 1705. The Duke was then already 55 years old. By the time the palace was finished some 17 years later, he was senile and on his deathbed, his Duchess Sarah was ready to scream at the mention of Blenheim, and the architect had walked out in a huff. But between them they had created perhaps the world's most perfect Baroque palace – perfectly splendid or perfectly dreadful, according to taste. The overall impact is enormous, the detailing beyond belief; as a prolonged yell of victory Blenheim has no equal. Capability Brown later laid out the gardens, planting trees to represent the disposition of troops at the Battle of Blenheim, and damming the River Glyme to create a lake. John Churchill stands in effigy on his Victory Column halfway down the avenue, dressed as a Roman general. Grebes, swans and dabchicks nest on the lake, happily dressed as themselves.

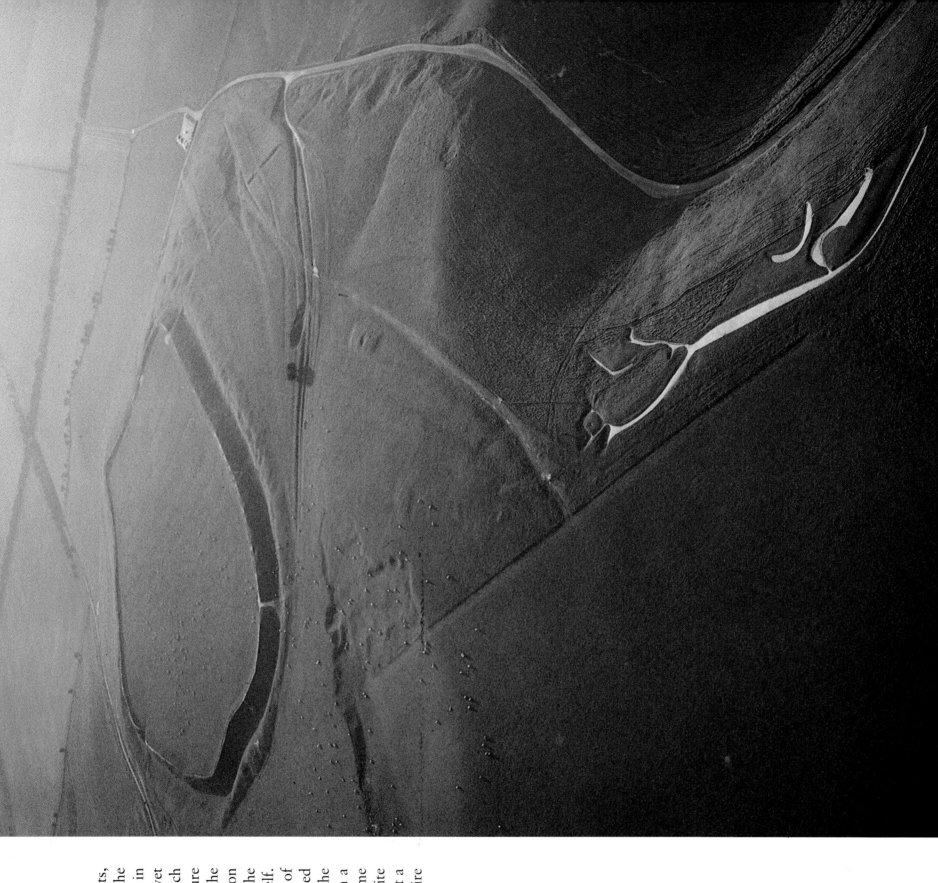

Uffington Castle, Oxfordshire

Berkshire has been reshaped at the whim of bureaucrats, but these rolling green hills remain for everyone the Berkshire Downs – even though they are now in Oxfordshire. Here is country where sheep and velvet pastures live together, creating and re-creating each other in harmony. The ground scars readily, for pure chalk lies but a spade's depth beneath the velvet, and the scars of ancient fortifications persist. Here is Uffington Castle, an Iron Age hill fort on the highest point of the Downs, with its outer ditch dug into the chalk itself. Ancient tracks show up too. Nearby (top left) is part of the Ridgeway, one of the oldest routes in Britain, used when the land below was heavily forested and only the Downs were passable. Ancient art also persists, with a little help from local enthusiasts who weed it from time to time. On the hillside below is the Uffington White Horse. No smug whisky advertisement horse this, but a wild horse-goddess that has careered over the Berkshire Downs perhaps since the fourth century BC.

Ashdown House, Ashbury, Oxfordshire

Like a five-storey Victorian dolls' house with hinged front and lid, Ashdown House stands on the Berkshire Downs between Ashbury and Lambourn. Except for its two pavilions and a farm building near by, it is entirely alone in a small formal garden with an avenue of well-ordered trees. Ashdown was built in vaguely Dutch style by William, the First Earl of Craven, about 1665. He dedicated it to the hapless sister of Charles 1, Queen Elizabeth of Bohemia, who died before she could make use of it. William lived in it until his own death some 35 years later. Ashdown remained in the Craven family until 1956, when it was presented to the National Trust. The house is built around a huge, beautifully-proportioned staircase and contains many portraits of the Queen and her Bohemian circle.

Henley-on-Thames, Oxfordshire

From its origins up in the Cotswolds the Thames is a winding old river, seldom striking in any one direction for more than a few hundred metres. Here at Henley-on-Thames it runs straight for nearly two kilometres (the Fair Mile), and that gave someone the idea, more than 150 years ago, of holding rowing and sailing races. The first Oxford and Cambridge boat-race was held at Henley in 1829, and ten years later came the first annual regatta. In 1851 Prince Albert lent his patronage, and the Royal Henley Regatta, held during the first week of July, became an event in the London season. The course is approximately 2,100 metres long, officially one mile and 25 furlongs. Although the regatta has no official status in international rowing, it is generally recognized as an important event and attracts good crews from overseas. Here we drift over the little market town and look straight down the Fair Mile. The bridge is a late-eighteenth-century creation, the church alongside is an earlier flint-and-stone parish church – like the town itself, comfortable but of no great distinction. Bunting and river markers, marquees and car parks, make it clear that this is Regatta week, and there will be Pimms and strawberries and cream in abundance under the awnings on the river-banks.

Eton College, Eton, Berkshire

Across the river from Slough, a stone's throw from Windsor, the tiny town of Eton nestles quietly by the Thames as it has done for centuries. Pleasant as it is, it could well have remained obscure – like the neighbouring villages of Boveney and Horton – had Henry VI not planted a small school there in 1440. The College began as a foundation of 70 young scholars – male, of course – who received free board and education. There was provision too for 20 other students, called Oppidans, who paid fees and were accommodated in houses and inns about the village. The first building (now called Lower School, and still in everyday use) was ready by 1443 – part of it forms the left-hand side of the quadrangle (known as School Yard). Lupton's Tower was built in 1520, and Upper School completed the quadrangle more than a century later. Today Eton College has a roll of over 1,100, and takes in many other buildings, including those immediately below us.

Woking, Surrey

Woking straddles the railway as other towns straddle a
high street. There was little enough there when the lines
from London to the south-west were laid through
wooded Surrey countryside in the 1830s. Then the sleepy
village of Woking, with its eleventh-century church and a
mention in the Domesday Book, suddenly found itself
landed with a railway station and a junction. Discover-
ing a new role for itself, it became a dormitory and
industrial centre less than an hour's run from Waterloo.
Here is a part of the dormitory – pleasant villas from the
1920s onward, their gardens mature, their swimming-
pools shades of azure, their real estate values spiralling
upwards as we swing lazily over them.

Scotney Castle, Lamberhurst, Kent

In the mid-to-late fourteenth century, Anglo-French relationships had reached a low ebb. The British were making clear their intent to hold Calais, and the French were expressing their anger and frustration by attacking the Isle of Wight and the ports of Winchelsea and Rye. Prudent citizens of the southern counties looked to the possibility of invasion, strengthening town walls and practising their swordsmanship. Rural landowners as well took stock, many of them fortifying their houses and barns. Close to the village of Lamberhurst, on the Kent-Sussex border, Roger Ashburnham dammed a small stream to create a moat, encircling two islands. On the islands he built a small but business-like castle, with curtain walls and four round towers – a castle big enough to hold his family and some of the neighbouring farmers with their stock. The French did not attack and Scotney Castle was gradually turned into a more comfortable manor house in the seventeenth century, and a section of the manor is still lived in today. The grounds around, including quarries, have been extensively landscaped, making a colourful setting for a tiny historical gem.

Bedgebury Pinetum, Goudhurst, Kent

Close to the southern border of Kent, the Royal Botanic Gardens at Kew and the Forestry Commission have together established a National Pinetum. This is a living museum and testing ground for pine trees of all kinds. It was started in 1924 and now has over 200 species, many dozens of varieties and a wide selection of non-coniferous trees as well. Some are individual standard trees, some grow in blocks to check their commercial value. There are stands and avenues of wellingtonias, Californian redwoods, Chilean pines, firs, yews, junipers and many other species. The Pinetum is open to the public, and has many well-planned walks, and there are good guide books for those who want to know more about pines.

Dover, Kent

Dover-to-Calais has always been the shortest and most direct route from Britain to the Continent, though wind and tide do not make it the easiest. The hill above, ringed with ancient earthworks, was a fort before the Romans arrived. The Romans improved it, called it Dubris, and built a lighthouse that could be seen far up the Channel. That is the stump of the lighthouse, standing by the western end of the little Anglo-Saxon church. The Normans too recognized the value of Dover. The massive keep and inner wall of their castle date from the twelfth century. The outer wall was added later, after an unsuccessful attack by the French in 1216. Still with a French invasion in mind, the castle was strengthened further during the eighteenth century and a warren of tunnels and chambers built under it was extended to accommodate troops. In the woodland behind Louis Bleriot landed his 25 horsepowered monoplane in July 1909 – the first cross-channel flight in a heavier-than-air machine, less than a lifetime ago.

Canterbury, Kent

There was already a village of settlers from the Low Countries on this site, beside a ford over the River Stour, when the Romans arrived. The Romans were quick to seize and fortify it, as always building strongly with foundations that still support parts of the existing wall. Angles, Saxons and Jutes moved in as the Romans left, and Augustine, on his mission from Rome in 597, found a well-established community with Ethelbert, its King, ripe for conversion. The Normans in turn saw the advantages of Canterbury and its splendid site, and in 1070 the first Norman Archbishop founded the cathedral on a mound where two previous churches had stood. Canterbury was already the most important centre for the Church in England when, in 1170, Archbishop Thomas à Becket was martyred close to the altar steps. Then it became a shrine for pilgrims and penitents to visit, with a flourishing tourist industry to cater for their needs. Canterbury is still one of Britain's major tourist attractions. Here we see it from the south, the town centre protected by a ring-road (immediately below us) that follows the old walls. The cathedral stands clear at the top of the picture, with the Whitstable to Dover road cutting across below it. The Stour meanders through the city, passing under the ring-road between the two roundabouts (bottom left).

Westbere, Kent

Crop-marks, the archaeologists call them, and sometimes they have much to tell. Old fields may show sites
of abandoned villages, Iron Age fortifications or ridge-
and-furrow patterns from medieval times. Sometimes the
sites of villas or granaries stand out, marked by a pattern
of post-holes. Often the track of an ancient road
continues across a field, while the modern road winds
sedately round the edge. Here are the wheel-marks of
cultivation impressed like tram-lines in the ripening
cereal, with a curious mottling of green – in this case
probably caused by channels of moisture in the subsoil.

Borough Green, Kent

The complex structure of the Weald makes for a wide
variety of soils and climates. Practically all of them are
good; it is just a matter of what crop can most profitably
be grown where. Here in Borough Green, on the south-
eastern outskirts of London, the traditional crops are
hops for beer-making and fruit for the London market.
The hops grow on tall vines, strung from poles that criss-
cross the fields (see p. 157). Traditionally the Cockneys
turned out from London's East End every summer for a
working holiday hop-picking, and the hop flowers were
dried in oast-houses like the ones at the bottom of the
picture. Spring brings the fruit blossom. This is the time
of year when Kent most clearly earns its 'Garden of
England' title, though there's another blossom-bedecked
garden just like it in the west too.

Pleshey, Essex

In the heart of rural Essex, between Chelmsford and Great Dunmow, this little village provides a direct link with ancient Normandy. The hill in the middle is a perfectly shaped motte (castle mound) 18 metres (60 feet) high, the foundation of a wooden keep built by a Norman landowner some nine centuries ago. The platform beside it is the bailey or inner defence, complete with mounded edge and moat. Surrounding the village is the ditch, almost 1½ kilometres (about a mile) long, that together with a thickly-laid hedge made up the outer perimeter. The village gets its name from this well-preserved set of defences; a *plaissiet* in Old French is a park or enclosure surrounded by a plashed hedge – one with branches interwoven to make it impassable. Surprisingly, Pleshey has never outgrown its perimeter, and never had cause to destroy its splendid medieval legacy.

Little Gaddesden, Hertfordshire

Drifting at leisure over Britain on tranquil autumn days, old-time balloonists and pilots would savour the sweet scent of burning leaves, wafting up perhaps from a garden bonfire. Today they are more likely to be kippered by clouds of smoke from burning stubble – acrid, pervasive smoke that hangs in the atmosphere for days. Every autumn after the combine harvesters have done their work, the fields are left full of unwanted stubble and straw, both in the way of the next operation in the farmer's busy calendar. So they are fired. Good farmers plough fire-breaks to protect hedges and trees, and burn only when they can keep the fires under control. There is some careful burning going on here; it needs to be, for those plantations beyond the farmhouse would light up merrily, given half a chance.

Waddesdon Manor, Buckinghamshire

Like other members of his wealthy family, Baron Ferdinand de Rothschild built himself a dream castle in the heart of rural Britain, his adopted country. Ferdinand's site was a hilltop in the Chilterns, close to the Buckinghamshire village of Waddesdon. He decapitated the hill, imported mature trees to create an instant forest, and built – of all things – Britain's most elegant French château. Born in Paris in 1839, Ferdinand married at 26. His young wife Evelina died in childbirth just 18 months later, and Ferdinand wandered across Europe for almost a decade before finally settling in 1874 and starting to build his home. French architects, designers and workmen shaped the Manor, and Ferdinand filled every room with exquisite French furnishings of the eighteenth century. He had no children and did not remarry; he became the local squire, Justice of the Peace, and Member of Parliament, dividing his time between Waddesdon, two other country houses and a town house in Piccadilly. He died in 1898 after one of his regular visits to Evelina's grave. Now Waddesdon is National Trust property, a museum, and a sad, splendid memorial to a lonely man.

Chequers Court, Buckinghamshire

Between High Wycombe and Aylesbury, about three kilometres (nearly two miles) east of Princes Risborough, stands the country residence of the British Prime Minister, surrounded by a large estate and a strong but unobtrusive security network. Chequers began as a small manor house in the thirteenth century, but was substantially rebuilt as a country mansion in the sixteenth century. In 1917 it was presented to the nation by Viscount Lee of Fareham. His intention was to provide a retreat where prime ministers could get away from the pressures of office. So it has been used by a succession of grateful Premiers and their guests since 1921. The house contains an interesting collection of Cromwell relics, but it is not open to the public.

Hampton Court, Greater London

Follow the Thames south-westward from London to Kingston and just beyond. As the river swings north, on the right hand bank stands Cardinal Wolsey's creation – Hampton Court Palace. There is no way of describing it in a few dozen words. It is a splendid four-square Tudor palace, remodelled with impeccable taste by Sir Christopher Wren in the seventeenth century. To be believed it must be seen and felt, for very few relics of Britain's past have come down to us so utterly unscathed. Wolsey began the palace about 1514 and presented it unfinished to his royal master Henry VIII. Henry enlarged it and used it as his main residence near London. William III commissioned Wren to revitalize Hampton Court, together with Bushy Park, which was part of its estate. The palace we see today is essentially Wren's concept of how an ancient royal residence should look. Royalty forsook it in Hanoverian times, and Hampton Court, with its fine collection of paintings, weapons and furniture, is now open for everyone to see and enjoy.

City of London, London

The City is the financial heartland of London, centred about St Paul's Cathedral, the Guildhall and the Bank of England on the north bank of the Thames. Devastated by fire in 1666 it arose from its ashes and carried on. Devastated again by bombing in World War II, it again recovered, this time in the modern idiom of steel, concrete and glass that has made it look startlingly like every other post-war city in the world. However, some of the old gems remain. Here on the right is St Paul's Cathedral, surely the most satisfying building in Britain. Up to it runs Ludgate Hill; beyond are Cheapside and Cannon Street in parallel. In the foreground are the green-domed Central Criminal Court – the Old Bailey – the Post Office depot with its red vans, and St Bartholomew's Hospital (left). Above is London Wall with the Barbican complex along the left-hand margin. Tower Bridge stands proudly on the river, with London Bridge in front of it and HMS Belfast moored between.

The Pool of London

The Heart of London

London Road, Rochester, 1938.

The Front, Brighton, 1932.

Derby Day traffic, 1921.

Blackpool Tower and Promenade, 1920.

Hop fields and steam engines, Kent, 1936.

Pottery kilns at Hanley, date unknown.

Colliers loading in Barry Docks, 1921.

Manchester, Central Library and city, 1937.

Marble Arch, London; procession for the Prince of Wales, 1922.

St Paul's and the City of London, 1939.

Crystal Palace after the fire, 1936.

The new Wembley Stadium after the Cup Final, 1923.

Mr Hearn wing-walking, 1932.

Early Aerofilms sortie, 1919.

Airship *R101* over Bayswater, London, 1929.

Sir Alan Cobham's flying circus, including an Aerofilms' aircraft, 1933.

Index of Illustrations